PLAYGROUND JUSTICE:

A Daughter's Nightmare,
A Town's Shame,
A Parent's Fight for Justice

By Mark and Debra Wein, with Rusty Fischer

PublishAmerica
Baltimore

© 2003 by Mark and Debra Wein, with Rusty Fischer.
All rights reserved. No part of this book may be reproduced, stored in a retrieval system, or transmitted in any form or by any means without the prior written permission of the publishers, except by a reviewer who may quote brief passages in a review to be printed in a newspaper, magazine, or journal.

First printing

ISBN: 1-4137-0033-0
PUBLISHED BY PUBLISHAMERICA, LLLP
www.publishamerica.com
Baltimore

Printed in the United States of America

TABLE OF CONTENTS

Prologue: *A Daughter's Nightmare*
In excruciating detail, a day in Mandi's elementary school life is painstakingly recreated for readers who could never imagine the torturous experience for themselves. From tying her shoes before school to drying her tears at the end of the day, witness a brave young girl's fight for survival in a world that should have been as safe as her very own home.

The language might be shocking, the violence R-rated, the pain all-too-real. But if it's unsettling for you, just think what it must have felt like for a seven-year-old girl clinging to her lunchbox like a lifeline — and turning to teachers, counselors, principals, and school board officials who over and over again refused to help the innocent little girl who just wanted to enjoy her first day of school...

Chapter One: *The Wheels on the Bus Go Round and Round...*
Mark and Debra Wein are glad when the new school year starts in their peaceful, tranquil hometown of Jefferson, Rhode Island. Their seven-year-old daughter Mandi is looking forward to it as well. Finally freed from the reigns of kindergarten, Mandi looks forward to her first day of first grade, where she'll finally be a "big kid" for once.

But as the Weins go blissfully school shopping, frantically buying new school shoes or hunting down items on their "school list" from Mandi's new first grade teacher at East Jefferson Elementary School, little do they know that their daughter is enjoying "the calm before the storm..."

Chapter Two: *First Grade*
At last! Mandi Wein is a first grader. Waking up early and rushing through her morning cereal, Mandi waves to Mark and Debra as she gleefully trots down to the local bus stop to await that golden chariot with the rest of her cherubic schoolmates. But from the very moment

she sets foot on her classmates' soil, Mandi quickly realizes that first grade is not going to be as fun, nor as innocent, as she thought.

Almost immediately, Mandi is pushed, shoved, called names, and verbally abused by a ruthless group of fourth and fifth grade boys who easily persuade the rest of the assembled schoolchildren to join along. Within minutes, Mandi's entire school year flashes before her eyes: name calling, violence, shame, remorse, humiliation, and abuse. And as the spit wads and rubber bands continue to fly once she boards the bus, and throughout the rest of that excruciatingly long school day, Mandi can only think ruefully: "One day down, 179 days to go…"

Chapter Three: *Warning Signs*

From that very first day, despite Mandi's hesitance to "tattle" on her fellow schoolmates, Mark and Debra Wein know that their youngest child is unhappy. Her clothes are rumpled, her hair's a mess, and her silence is uncharacteristic for a seven-year-old girl who only eight hours earlier was ecstatic to start her first year in "real school."

But as first grade progresses, that first, shocking day is less of a rarity — and more of a death knell for tiny little Mandi Wein. Day after day, week after week, Mandi is physically and emotionally abused at the hands of her young classmates. From schoolyard abuse to cafeteria warfare, nowhere is safe for the Weins' daughter. And despite their almost *daily* complaints to Mandi's teachers, counselors, and even her principal, Mandi is destined to spend an entire year at the mercy of schoolchildren so vicious that their scathing and vindictive epithets can't even be repeated here.

Chapter Four: *How Can It Go On?*

After a too-short summer free of the torture of school and full of childhood innocence, Mandi and the Weins brace themselves for another long school year at East Jefferson Elementary School. Although distrustful of the teachers, counselors, and administration at school, the Weins have to believe that this year will be better. That someone will listen. That someone will care. That somehow, some way, their daughter Mandi will be safer in her second grade classroom than she was back in first grade.

Safe from the staples and the spit wads and the rubber bands and the paper clips. Safe from the name calling and the spitting and the hair pulling and the shame. But from day one, Mandi feels a nauseating sense of déjà vu as she is immediately and relentlessly assaulted at her very own bus stop, on the bus, and throughout her first long day of second grade. Again, all Mandi and the Weins can do is hope. Hope and pray that this year, please God, that this year not be a repeat of first grade…

Chapter Five: *Second Grade*

One week into the school year and already the pattern is the same: Mandi is repeatedly assaulted, sometimes physically, at the bus stop, on the bus, and throughout the long school day. Debra, hearing the trials and tribulations of her innocent eight-year-old daughter, then makes her daily call to the administrative offices at East Jefferson Elementary School.

All in vain. Again and again, over and over, day after day, Debra's and Mark's repeated attempts to get someone, *anyone* to listen to their complaints about their daughter's treatment fall on deaf ears. Teachers look the other way, counselors offer pat, pedantic one-liners that read more like bumper stickers, and the principal is clearly already tired of the intrusion to his daily school routine. But one thing motivates the Weins to keep after their daughter's teachers, counselors, and administrators: the thought of their eight-year-old daughter being called names, punched, and kicked for eight hours a day, five days a week, all year long…

Chapter Six: *Third Grade*

Another blissful summer. Another "first day of school." This time — third grade. Mandi is older now: nine years old, to be exact. And Mark and Debra feel not only older, but wiser as well. This year, they know, someone will have to listen. This year, they know, will not be the same. This year, they know, Mandi will be safe.

But again, like a third strike in the most important baseball game of their entire lives, Mandi's abuse continues right where it left off the minute she plants her timid feet on the bus stop sand. The abuse continues, as always, on the bus and in the classroom. Powerless to defend herself against the bigger kids, let alone the sheer number of kids, who pick on her like sharks swirling around a bloody feeding frenzy, Mandi can do little more than complain to the grown-ups at her school. But again, like history repeating itself, no one is there to listen to the bruised and battered third grader…

Chapter Seven: *"Help us, please!"*

For once and for all, the Weins are fed up with their daughter's systematic abuse at East Jefferson Elementary School. When told of their daughter's continued abuse at the bus stop and on the bus, naïve and perhaps uncaring school officials tell Debra Wein to simply drive her daughter to school.

But despite the brief respite from her bus stop and bus riding torturers, Mandi's abuse continues almost immediately the moment she sets foot inside the school halls after her mom drops her off for yet another torturous day at school. From classroom to classroom, in the library, in the gym, on the PE field, in the cafeteria, Mandi's abusers are nothing if not cunning in finding new ways to torture the young third grader to make up for the time they lost not abusing her on the bus!

Chapter Eight: *Mandi's Lost Year*

The plot thickens as third grade unfolds, the abuse continues, and the Weins bombard the Jefferson County School Board with complaints about their daughter's treatment at East Jefferson Elementary. But if the frazzled family of four thought they might get some help from the next level in the chain of command, they were severely mistaken.

Again, the Weins are given the run-around — this time only by men in better suits. More excuses, more denials, and more repetition of the word "overreacting" than Mark and Debra can bear to recall.

No longer able to send their daughter off to a public school that is not only unsafe — but worse, un*caring* — the Weins do the formerly unthinkable and pull Mandi out of East Jefferson Elementary to put her in a local private school where her slate will be clean, her days unsullied by violence, torture, and shame.

Chapter Nine: *Judgment Day*

Seeking counsel while Mandi enjoys a temporary reprieve from her torturers at private school, the Weins are determined to get justice for their battered and abused daughter. Hearing their case, attorney Charles D. Sylvester agrees to take their case — all the way to the Supreme Court if necessary.

Filing complaints against, and eventually suing, not only the Jefferson County School Board but both of Mandi's former principals at East Jefferson Elementary School, the Weins make history by being the first parents ever to file a civil case against a Rhode Island school board for physical and emotional abuse. But it certainly doesn't win the devoted family of four any popularity contests with the locals...

Chapter Ten: *Order in the Court?*

Unfortunately, a strong case for the Weins doesn't necessarily translate into "the most popular" award in the tiny town of Jefferson, Rhode Island. Seen as a threat to the Jefferson County School Board, the police department, and a way of life that has succeeded unimpeded for decades, the Weins are soon cast in the role of public enemy number one in both local print and media.

But not everyone is against them. Facts are facts, and the Weins have nothing to gain from suing the Jefferson County School Board except seeing justice served for their emotionally crippled daughter Mandi, who is already beginning to show signs of Post-Traumatic Stress Syndrome, or PTSD.

Chapter Eleven: *The Verdict*

The trial of the Weins vs. the Town of Jefferson was narrowly averted when lawyers for the Jefferson County School Board decided to settle with the Weins before a costly — and potentially damaging — jury trial was set to begin. Though lawyers for the school board downplay *which* of the six figures the court awarded the Weins, one thing is clear: culpability was proven in a case that never went to court.

But "winning" is a word the Weins would never use to describe their verdict in the case of their daughter versus the school board. Scorned by their community, threatened at home, parents of a daughter forever scarred by her experiences in the Jefferson County School System, the Weins are reluctant heroes to a small but loyal community of educators devoted to seeing safe schools — and children safe at school.

Conclusion: *Justice for Mandi?*

While their settlement was admittedly in the high six-figures, the Weins obviously feel that justice has been denied their abused daughter, who now suffers not only from post-traumatic stress disorder but obsessive compulsive disorder as well as a result of the abuse she suffered at the hands of every day American schoolchildren like those we pass at the bus stop every single day.

Now home schooling their daughter to shelter her from additional abuse she may suffer through retribution from local schoolchildren — and school officials — alike, the Weins plan a move to sunny Florida to entirely remove little Mandi from a town that now sees the entire family as a pox on their community, even though the Weins have personally seen to it that, hopefully, no such schoolyard abuse will ever occur in Jefferson, Rhode Island again!

SCHOOL BUSES

"School bus transportation should be treated as a privilege, not a right, and is an extension of the school system. A Student's misconduct at a bus stop or while on a bus may provide sufficient reason to discontinue providing bus service for a specific amount of time. Children are expected to ride only on the bus to which they are regularly assigned, and to get on and off at their proper bus stops. If it becomes necessary to deviate from this routine, parents must request, in writing, permission from the principal. A copy of the Bus Rules and Regulations will be given to each student during the first month of school."

~ **Jefferson Public Schools**, *Handbook for Elementary Students and Parents*

INTRODUCTION:
How Did it Come to This?

Jonesboro, Arkansas. Columbine High School. Pearl, Mississippi. What do all of these horrific — and instantly recognizable — school shootings have in common? Bullying. Like algebra or spelling lists, PE or pep rallies, schoolyard bullying has become a daily ritual at elementary schools across the nation. From verbal abuse to physical assaults, from badgering to battery, the cases of schoolyard bullying are nothing short of a national epidemic. In fact, the most recent Bureau of Justice statistics concerning *School Crime and Safety* estimates that "one out of four school-aged children is bullied."

For three long, painful, arduous years, little Mandi Wein *was* that "one out of four" unfortunate children. From first grade through third — almost *half* of her entire elementary school existence — Mandi endured a systematic pattern of abuse that defies not only the imagination — but sours the stomach. From epithets too vulgar to repeat here to violent physical abuse including scratching, punching, pushing, and even skewering with a sharpened number-2 pencil, Mandi endured a living hell that lasted until her parents, Mark and Debra, were forced to pull her out of Jefferson Elementary School and pay for her to go to a nearby private school.

Despite repeated attempts to inform authorities in the Jefferson Department of Schools, including the principal at Mandi's school, her teachers, her counselors, the school board, and eventually the Jefferson Police department itself, Mandi's abuse continued unabated.

Mornings became a torturous ritual of dread, nausea, and an endless litany of excuses from poor Mandi to stay home. Visits to the bus stop became painfully violent at the hands of her torturers, young schoolchildren barely out of training pants themselves. A ride aboard the school bus each morning became a daily gauntlet of hurled staples, paper clips, epithets, rubber bands, and spit wads. And by the time she finally got to school, the kids were just getting started!

For poor little Mandi Wein, school became less of a haven, and more of a nightmare...

The sad truth is, Mandi Wein is not alone: According to the Bureau of Justice, a child is bullied *every seven minutes*. Consider these other sobering statistics:

1 out of 5 kids admits to being a bully, or doing some "bullying"

8% of students miss 1 day of class per month for fear of bullies

43% fear harassment in the bathroom at school

100,000 students carry a gun to school

28% of youths who carry weapons have witnessed violence at home

282,000 students are physically attacked in secondary schools each month

80% of the time, an argument with a bully *will* end up in a physical fight

1/3 of students surveyed said they heard another student threaten to kill someone

85% of schoolyard bullying persists without intervention from either teachers or other students

And America has had enough...

FOR THE CHILDREN ...
Putting a Stop to Schoolyard Abuse

WHAT EXACTLY *IS* BULLYING?

Children's safety is often one of parents' main concerns. Parents today hope that their children are safe at home, at school and at the playground. Despite the best precautions, there are rare cases in which your child could be a victim of bullying. The following recommendations may help your child if he is being bullied, or prevent your child from ever becoming a victim to bullies. These recommendations will also give you tips to detect if your child is being bullied and will suggest basic behaviors that can help your child.

What *is* bullying? If a youth or a gang at school steals goods or money from your child, is insulting or shows contempt, threatens or hits your child, or forces him to do things against his will, then it's called *bullying*. These incidents used to be rare, but are becoming more and more common as overburdened schools become more and more lax in their discipline policies, and your child could become a victim.

PROLOGUE:
A Daughter's Nightmare

It wasn't a long walk to the bus stop. Not a long walk at all. Besides, the bus stop was where all the big kids hung out. The second graders. The third graders. Even some of the fourth and fifth graders! And, on her first ever day of first grade at East Jefferson Elementary School, the little girl was ready to be a "big kid."

Finally…

The little girl's mom wanted to walk with her, watch over her, protect her, but she didn't want to embarrass her on her first day. Didn't want the rest of the kids to laugh at her when she and her mom showed up, hand in hand, when all of the rest of the kids were old enough to walk to the bus stop alone.

So the little girl waved goodbye to her mommy and walked the short way to the bus stop. Alone. Like a big girl. Despite her brave little face, however, there were butterflies in her stomach all the way there. To distract herself, she listened carefully to the sound of her new school shoes scuff the pavement as she walked and wondered what all of the other little girls would be wearing for their first day of school.

The little girl looked back fondly on the special shopping days she had shared with her mommy, just the two of them, as summer drew to a close and the first day of school finally neared. They'd searched all over town for just the right school clothes for a big, grown-up first grader like herself. None of the silly pink kitty cat jumpers or light-up sneakers she'd worn in kindergarten. She was a big girl now and she needed just the right clothes to make a good first impression.

For a brief, stolen moment, just as she rounded the corner and approached the bustling bus stop, where kids even earlier than she was were already assembled and laughing gaily and joking playfully, the little girl secretly wished that it *wasn't* the first day of school already. Wished that she and her mommy could be back in the mall, shopping for clothes at store after store and taking one of their many breaks for lemonade or a hot slice of pizza or, if she were *really* good, an ice cream cone!

All of a sudden, the little girl missed her mommy. Missed her warm, cozy bed and her nice, safe room and all the sleepy, peaceful dozing she'd done over the warm, sweet summer. Like nervous school kids everywhere on this eventful day of days, the little girl was torn between growing up — and sleeping *in*!

But just as quickly, the moment passed and the little girl felt a spring in her step as she skipped the rest of the way to the bus stop, not caring if her new school shoes scuffed or not. Skip, skip, skip. Almost there now. Skip, skip, skip. Recognizing faces of the neighborhood kids she already knew. Skip, skip, skip. Finally. It was official.

The little girl was a big kid! Standing at the bus stop with the rest of the big kids. Proud of her new school clothes. Waving to her little friends. All but shouting, "Look at me. I'm in first grade. I'm a big girl now!"

And, for a moment, her celebration could last. Things went fine. At first. The big kids ignored her, her little neighborhood friends from kindergarten greeted her warmly with squeals of delight and shared nervousness. There was kiddy gossip to share, new rubberized Trapper Keepers with the zippers and buttons and hidden pockets to show off, shiny shoes to "ooh" and "aah" over. There were giggles. Smiles. Perhaps even a hug or two.

But as the newness of seeing each other wore off, a stuffy silence slowly crept between the messy gaps between "oohs" and "aahs." First the little kids felt it, then the bigger kids, then the *really* big kids. They felt the silence, the fidgeting, the newness. And in the silence, in the fidgeting, in the newness, the big kids got bored. Real bored.

And in their boredom, as always, they looked for a victim...

Who knows why they chose her over all the rest of the little kids at the bus stop that day. She was a little girl like all the other little girls. Her face was no different, nor her hair nor her shape nor her teeth nor her legs. Her clothes were normal, her shoes were fine, she was as normal and happy and carefree a little girl as you could ever hope to find at a busy, crowded bus stop on the first day of school.

But in those uneasy few moments it took to find a victim, the big kids from fourth and fifth grade zeroed in on her with razor sharp insight and perfect, lethal cunning. Maybe she looked their way once too many times. Maybe she didn't look their way half enough. Maybe she wasn't as tall as the other girls, or just an inch *too* tall. Maybe she didn't laugh at their jokes soon enough, or perhaps she laughed too soon.

Either way, the little girl might as well have had a target painted on her back, her front, her top, her bottom. Like stealthy, guided missiles in backwards caps and baggy shorts, a gaggle of fourth and fifth grade boys gravitated to her without hesitation. Pushing other kids aside, edging forward, sending shared signals between each other like vultures swooping slowly over road kill. First they called her names. Loudly. So all the other children could hear them.

Then they called her some more names. Louder this time.

Much louder...

The little girl didn't know what to do. Didn't know how to react. Didn't know what to say, if she should say anything at all. Were they just playing around? These big kids with their dirty mouths and baggy pants? Was this all part of the first day of school for "little kids who want to be big kids" ritual? Were they trying to be her friends? Was this how they showed their friendship?

So, at first, the little girl laughed. Nervously. Her hand over her mouth, as if she didn't want to draw any more attention to herself than she already had. But like blood in the water, her nervous laughter only spurred the boys on, made them madder, hurt their already fragile egos, wounded their pride. So the name calling grew worse, more personal, more scathing, more evil. They made fun of her clothes, her new school clothes. Pointing. Laughing. Braying. They made fun of her hair, her face, her shape, her innocent little baby fat.

The quieter our little girl got, the louder they became. Like a game without rules, the pranks swirled wider and farther out of control. Closer and closer the pack of wild boys hovered, their gawky, outstretched arms swinging wilder and wilder, their knobby knees shaking with excitement, with violence, with betrayal.

They kicked up sand with their too-big shoes, spit when they shouted, their faces erupting into maniacal masks of petulant glee as again and again they degraded the girl with their foul mouths and immaturity. As the school bus neared they instinctively felt the play clock ticking out of time, their antic escalating wildly out of control. Closer. Harder. Faster. Meaner.

She held it in. All of it. Our brave little girl. She reigned in the fear and the panic and the drama and the chaos and held it all together until that glorious yellow school bus finally came. When it arrived, when it spared her, momentarily anyway, from her merciless tormentors, she hopped on eagerly, whispering with her little friends and sensing relief and just glad that it was all over. That it was finally done.

That it had ended...

And, for just a moment, as the driver tipped his cap and welcomed her and her little friends to their first day of school and waited until all the little children in his car were safely seated before pulling away from the horrible little bus stop, the little girl thought, she truly believed, that it *was* over.

But as that merciless pack of fourth and fifth grade boys, now recruiting reinforcements from the other kids on the bus and growing exponentially in number, slowly circled around her, sitting behind her, sitting beside her, sitting in front of her, she knew that it was far from over, that it had only just begun.

As the little girl's timid, bashful eyes caught the furtive glance of the already nervous bus driver in the big rearview mirror, there was one last glimmer of hope. He could stop this. He could take it all away. He could pull the bus over and put the fear of God into these evil little boys and that would be the end of it. For now. Forever...

But, instead, the only grown-up for miles and miles caught her glance, winced, and looked quickly, furtively away. As if he was thinking, *Eyes on the road. Eyes on the road. Look straight ahead. Don't look back. The ride will be over soon. Then the teachers can take over. Or the counselors. Or the principal. It's none of my business. I'm not in charge. Heck, I only make 8 bucks an hour. Let someone else handle it!*

The boys saw it. So did our little girl. So did her friends. So did everyone else on the bus. It happened in a split second, and it changed the little girl's life. That one moment — the one moment that could have saved her, that could have rescued her — instead gave the boys on that bus, forever and all time, the feeling that it was okay.

That what they were doing was right. Okay, maybe not that it was *right*, but that it was right *enough*. That it was okay. That it was okay *enough* to pass under the bus driver's radar. That they wouldn't get in trouble for it. That it wouldn't get them kicked off the bus, or out of school, or even a detention.

The little girl lost all hope then...

In one brief, flickering moment, in the second it took for the bus driver to look away, to give up, all hope was lost. The boys pushed her, shoved her, pulled her onto their lap, whispered dirty things, nasty things, while all the while older girls called her names and pulled her hair and dissed her clothes, her shoes, her shape.

It was an orgy of violence, both perceived and acted upon. With no adult supervision, with no boundaries, with no recourse, with no rules, the bigger boys and girls aboard that ill-fated bus escalated into a muted pattern of violence that was straight out of *Lord of the Flies*. Like some careless lab experiment left unsupervised just five minutes too long, the lid was off and the game was on.

Testing, ever probing, the boys and girls aboard that bus held sway with a merciless little experiment of their own. Moments, then full minutes, passed and no one told them to stop. No one even raised their voice or intervened or warned them to be good. The pushed the limits, found no barriers in their path, and went beyond those few limits that they had even set for themselves.

They crossed a line, and kept on crossing until it was far, far behind them...

She never cried, our brave little girl. Not once. Even as the torment continued for mile after mile after mile. Even as the pranks grew nastier, more personal, more cruel. She never shed a tear, though her tiny little chin quivered and her powerless little hands trembled in a fear that might have crushed children twice her age. The whole way to school, through the gauntlet of pain and abuse and yelling and laughter and screaming, the girl had but one thought in her bewildered little brain.

One thought saw her through the torment.

One thought sealed her doom.

One day down, she thought to herself, holding back the tears that threatened to spill from her wounded doe eyes. *One day down and only 179 to go...*

FOR THE CHILDREN ...
Putting a Stop to Schoolyard Abuse

THE THREE FORMS OF BULLYING:

There are three ways children can be bullied:

Physical Bullying: This happens when your child is hit, pushed, has her hair pulled, and so on.

Verbal Bullying: This can be name calling, racist and sexist comments, foul language and includes unkind jokes, for example, about weight. Verbal bullying is the most frequent type and is very common for children aged nine to 13. Verbal bullying is not teasing — teasing happens when both the teaser and child are having fun and there is no plan to upset each other.

Relational Bullying: This means being left out or having nasty gossip passed around about you. Young children can suffer especially from this type of bullying.

CHAPTER ONE:
The Wheels on the Bus Go Round and Round...

The first day of school gratefully behind her, Mandi Wein rushed home the brief few yards from the offending bus stop and practically flung herself into the arms of her anxiously awaiting mother, Debra. Although she'd pledged to herself to remain strong, it wasn't long before Mandi began sobbing out her story in great, big, gulping breaths of air.

For her part, Debra could hardly believe her ears. She had spent all day imagining this very moment: Mandi's triumphant homecoming from her very first day of school. There were even fresh cookies and milk on the table, awaiting her daughter's first few minutes through the door. Debra had pictured the two of them sitting there in the sun-drenched kitchenette, Debra listening while Mandi went on and on about all her new friends.

What she was hearing from her daughter's trembling lips was miles away from anything she could have imagined for herself — *or* her precious little daughter. Debra had caught herself smiling often that day, caught up in some hazy daydream of Mandi's first day.

Mandi greeting the teacher. Mandi introducing herself to the rest of her class. Mandi falling in with a gaggle of other precocious first-graders in the cafeteria, munching away on her pudding cup or even trading precious desserts with the other girls. Mandi giggling energetically on the playground, jumping rope or hanging off jungle gyms with the rest of the girls. The memories of her own first day of first grade flooded back to Debra, causing even more smiles as the hands on the kitchen clock ticked slowly, ever so slowly, the minutes, then hours, of that long, fateful day.

Mandi was such a good-natured girl, a ray of light in all of their lives. Debra couldn't see how anyone wouldn't embrace her daughter the way most others did. Warmly. Openly. With love and friendship and compassion. Why, Debra had even made extra cookies, just in case Mandi had gotten overly excited and inadvertently invited all of her new girlfriends home with her!

Now the cookies lay there, looking almost obscene in their forced cheerfulness. Debra almost felt ashamed: here she'd been at home, safe and sound and surrounded by the comfort of her homey surroundings, while all the while Mandi had been pushed, shoved, and verbally and sexually assaulted by her own peers.

As Mandi slowly but surely calmed down, Debra drew more and more of the story out of her. The abuse, starting at the bus stop, continuing on the bus, and then escalating throughout the day until things grew violent, personal, and nasty.

Debra stepped back from Mandi and regarded her with the careful eye of a concerned mother. She nearly gasped, wondering how she hadn't recognized her blemished face, tousled hair, and rumpled clothes the minute she walked through the front door. Goofing around and roughhousing were one thing, but Mandi's disheveled appearance was a tell-tale sign that her day at school had been the longest one of her short, little life. While there were no bruises or scrapes or bloody noses, Debra could see that poor Mandi had been through something.

Something *bad*…

A day of celebration turned to a day of mourning as the rest of the family learned of Mandi's day-long ordeal. Her sisters were comforting, her father tried his best, but it naturally fell to Debra to rectify the situation and make things right for her precious little girl.

Mandi ate little that night at dinner, and talked even less. Her older sister, Jessica, bit her tongue and spared little Mandi the cheerful and funny anecdotes she could have so easily shared about her first day at the high school, where things had gone just swimmingly.

She didn't want to "rub it in."

After dinner, Debra watched as Mandi washed up and got ready for bed. The wounded little girl didn't even make a fuss when Debra turned off the TV and shushed her straight to bed. Even before she pulled the door shut, Debra could hear the unmistakable sniffling sounds of Mandi starting to cry herself to sleep.

Hours later, she joined her...

The next morning, after a fitful sleep, Debra watched Mandi carefully as she went about her morning routine. Shower. Clothes. Breakfast. Brushed teeth. Lunch bag. Backpack. There were papers to sign — permission slips and consent forms and other detritus of the first day of school — and before mother and daughter knew that it was time to rush to the bus stop.

Debra's stomach lurched as Mandi's face crumpled into a prelude to tears. She wanted to surmount this obstacle for her, take her place, step into her shoes and show those rowdy kids at school a thing or two. But it was every mother's eternal dilemma: do things for them, and court a life of unhealthy co-dependence. Let them do for themselves, and create strong, independent children who grow into strong, independent adults.

It had been a restless night for both of them, and the dark circles under their eyes were matching badges of their mutual worry and concern. From her second-story window, Debra could see the other children milling about the corner bus stop.

"Which ones?" Debra asked little Mandi.

Mandi didn't even hesitate. "That one," she practically whimpered, her tiny finger quivering as she pointed. "And that one, and him, too."

Debra nodded. The Mead* boys. All three of them: Rizzo*, Skeeter*, and Pugsley*. She should have guessed. Shaking herself now, Debra kissed Mandi on the cheek, double-checked her lunch and backpack, and watched solemnly from the front porch as Mandi walked slowly down the flight of stairs and across the street to the bus stop.

Even from across the street, Debra could feel the tension in the air as Mandi dragged her feet the whole way there. The Mead brothers put their heads together, obviously planning another frontal assault.

Debra sighed. She had hoped, she had wished, she had even prayed that Mandi's first day had been an aberration. That it had all been a fluke. That, God forgive her, those troublemakers and hoodlums would focus their attention on someone else, some other poor kid, on the second day of school.

But now Debra watched, aghast, as several children, both young and old and all lead by the Mead brothers, descended on Mandi with shouts and catcalls and pushes and shoves. Despite her firm insistence on staying out of it, Debra marched down to the bus stop and defended her daughter like a lioness defends her cub.

"Go mess with the other boys," she shouted to the Mead brothers, enraged by their insolent smirks and dirty faces. "Leave her alone. She's just a little girl!"

Debra dragged Mandi home and together they waited by the front stoop until the bus came. Then they walked across the street together and Debra warned the bus driver about what had happened, not just that morning, but the day before. He assured her that he would "take care of it."

Debra had no reason not to trust him. She made sure Mandi sat up front and breathed a sigh of relief. Her daughter had made it to the bus safely. It had taken her intervention, but she had made it. Now there were two adults, not just a bus driver but a paid bus monitor, to supervise the children and make sure nothing happened on the way to school.

She wasn't exactly rushing home to bake cookies, but Debra Wein ruefully allowed a strained smile to caress her lips as she watched the lazy yellow school bus lurch away from the corner and deliver her daughter to East Jefferson Elementary School.

And her second day of school...

On the bus, things weren't going quite as planned. That tends to happen, when the grown-ups go away. As the bus driver's stops multiplied, so did his little charges, and school board policy was that only the youngest children got to sit up front. As the tiny kindergartners piled on with their little shoes and adorable fuzzy backpacks, Mandi Wein, a first grader, was ordered to move farther back in the bus.

With hooded eyes and a growing sense of doom, Mandi — a good girl — did as she was told. Instantly, Skeeter Mead pulled her onto his seat with coarse language and crude innuendoes. As the bus bounced and the fifth grader's overactive hormones flared, he again and again pulled tiny little Mandi down onto his prepubescent lap.

His brothers laughed. So did his friends. So did his girlfriends. So did perfect strangers, boys, girls, good kids, bad kids, all of whom were too nervous — or too scared — to do anything else. Skeeter himself glared wildly at little Mandi, manhandling the tiny first grader and, perhaps without even knowing it, sexually assaulting her with his primitive actions and roughhousing turned obscene.

Mandi fought back as best she could, but was much too weak against the bigger, stronger boy — made fierce by the mob mentality that pervaded on the bus. His ploy was perfect: the minute the bus driver looked in his rearview mirror to see what all the ruckus was about, Mandi would be shoved onto the other side of the seat with Skeeter looking as innocent as an angel. The minute the adult looked away, back onto his lap Mandi would be dragged.

Over and over again the tiny first grader was violated, until finally the bus rolled to a stop and Skeeter's fun ended. But even the trip's end brought no closure to Mandi's torment: "See you on the ride home," the older boy grinned as he dashed off the bus with his gaggle of friends screaming with laughter at the fun to be had at the end of the day.

Mandi felt like crying, felt like tattling, felt like shouting to the rooftops, but even after only one day of school, even on her second day of first grade, she already knew the secret code of schoolchildren everywhere: Telling the adults will only make it worse!

Mandi trudged through the halls, wiping her eyes, drying her sniffly nose on her sleeve, straightening the cute pink skirt she and her mother had so carefully picked out for her on one of their many shopping trips for school clothes. Mandi's teacher, Mrs. Arnsbauch*, greeted her pleasantly, but all Mandi could do was mumble a solemn "good morning" in reply.

She was too young to give it a name, but still the irony of her situation wasn't lost on her: All around her adults stood. Big people. Smart people. Strong people. They smiled with their mouths, asked with their eyes, patted with their big, firm hands. But as able and willing and helpful as they might have seemed, a gulf as wide as the Grand Canyon itself separated them from their seemingly innocent young charges.

Logic would tell an adult that Mandi had every opportunity to ease herself out of her current situation. "Blow the whistle," they would shout from their easy chairs and Barcaloungers. "Tell on the kid. What's his name? Skeeter? Rat the kid out. You may not be voted Miss Popular afterward, but your bus stop troubles will surely be over."

But kids, even little kids, even the smallest of children, knew better. A hundred pairs of eyes were watching Mandi's every move. At the bus stop. On the bus. In the halls. On the playground. In the cafeteria. Before and after class. A dozen spies, a dozen Mead brother cronies, filled the hallways with their beady eyes and laconic grins.

From day one little Mandi had been marked, tagged, targeted, tested, and given the grand prize of all booby prizes. She was "it." She was the one. The one for all time. The whole, long, drawn-out school year. It was Mandi. Nothing she could do about it now.

Not when the bus drivers looked the other way. Not when the $6 an hour bus monitor was busy doing the newspaper crossword while spit wads and paper clips soared straight over her head. Not when Mandi's first-grade teacher had thirty other kids to hustle into class before first bell and couldn't find the time to notice one little girl's red-rimmed eyes, rumpled clothing, and trembling hands.

It's a modern fact of public school life. A hidden world that only gets talked about in the hazy, crazy days following a school shooting or bomb threats. Everyone knows it exists. The bullying. The threats. The implied violence. The mob mentality. The teachers. The parents. The principals. The school board. The media. The policy makers.

The lawmakers. The politicians.

But no one knows it better than the children themselves. Both the predators and the prey. Outside the brick walls and spotless windows, the modern American elementary school looks like something out of a Norman Rockwell painting. Even inside, with the halls clear of children and the lockers freshly painted, it's easy to find oneself reminiscing about the good old days and imagining a population of apple-cheeked, pigtailed children walking single file from class to class.

But dig a little deeper, scratch just beneath the surface, and the tension is as thick as London fog in winter. Bullies roam the halls, violent and ruthless. Not always bigger, not always smarter, not even always older, these instinctive predators prey on the weak, the young, the small, the naïve, the goofy, the silly.

Swirlies. Wedgies. Indian burns. Raspberries. Harmless pranks? Perhaps when viewed with the golden perspective of time — and age. But not when you're the one cornered in the bathroom, trying desperately to fight off four boys three grades above you who will stop at nothing short of dunking your head into a flushing toilet.

Harmless? How harmless is it to spend the next three hours drenched in urinal water as the news of what happened in first period races through the entire school of almost 700 children who will be giggling behind that poor boy's back for the rest of the school year?

One thing's for sure: 699 other kids breathed a huge sigh of relief when it was decided on only the second day of school that little Mandi Wein would be the scapegoat for the rest of the year. And none of them sighed any louder than the rest of the lowly first graders in Mandi's class.

It's a life few adults ever see. The trips. The falls. The pushes. The shoves. The whispered epithets and outright name calling that accompanies some children from the first bell to the last. Oh, sure. They hear rumors. "Ms. Goodson," some nerdy tattletale will whisper, "the kids are being mean to Mandi again."

But without proof, a teacher's hands are tied. Unless they actually see something, with their own two eyes, what can a teacher actually

do? And no one in an elementary school has more street smarts —
not the teachers, not the counselors, not the assistant principal, not
the principal — than the resident bully.

He or she will never let an adult see his devious ways, his actual
crimes. They might catch his less street wise henchmen, those three
or four hangers on and wannabes who follow the bully through the
school, doing his dirty work and taking his licks, all for the privilege
of hanging out with the baddest kid in school.

The resident bully is too smart for that.

Much too smart...

FOR THE CHILDREN ...
Putting a Stop to Schoolyard Abuse

"Nothing can prepare you for living...with a sociopathic serial bully. It is the most devastating, draining, misunderstood, and ultimately futile experience imaginable."
~ Tim Field, Author of **Tim Field**, Author of *Bullycide: Death at Playtime*

****

HOPE & HEALING CAN BE FOUND IN SUPPORT GROUPS

Violent crimes such as schoolyard abuse and playground bullying are naturally traumatizing to those individuals whose lives are touched by such aberrations of justice. The violent incident goes well beyond what we experience in normal daily life, and few of us are prepared to deal with it emotionally.

Emotional reactions can range from shock, numbness, and denial to outright hysteria and panic. The victim feeling alone and isolated, like no one truly understands what he or she has been through, often accompanies the trauma. Family members of victims experience very similar reactions, such as in the case of homicide victims. Many crime victims and their family members have found hope through developing a network of friends sharing similar experiences in support groups.

The following list provides some insight into the many benefits of support group involvement:

Emotional healing comes when people interact with other people.
Sharing of similar experiences helps members feel less alone and more ready to deal with day-to-day issues.

Encouragement comes from learning about how others have conquered situations similar to theirs.

Contribution helps support group members feel meaningful.

Education results from the exposure to information and personal experiences in a group.

Socialization occurs when connections with people are made and confidence in social skills develops when appropriate interaction occurs in support groups.

Self-expression, as emotions are experienced and released, creates a greater understanding of oneself.

Confidence building results as members take responsibility for the work of the group, and see progress with the plans they made.

Safety, in the environment of a confidential, supportive, non-judgmental group, allows for honest disclosure and sharing of common difficulties.

A sense of growth occurs as long-term members see new participants and reminiscence about where they began and how far they have come in their personal journey.

*(**Source**: 1999 Brain Injury Association of Minnesota)*

CHAPTER TWO:
First Grade

In one short week, five quick days, Mandi Wein's little life became a living hell that would be hard for most adults to imagine — let alone endure. An unseen target painted squarely upon her tiny back, for what exact reason no one will ever know, her destiny as a first grader is irretrievably linked with those bullies, thugs, and hoodlums who would had liked nothing better than to see her crawl under a rock and stay there for the rest of the school year.

But Mandi Wein, like most young children of school age, has been taught *exactly* what to do when bad kids hassle good ones. In a hundred different venues, she's heard the same warning message repeated over and over again. From libraries to rec centers, DARE programs to pre-school, the same American mantras are repeated over and over again:

"Stop, Drop & Roll!"

"Never take candy from strangers!"

"Just say NO to Drugs!"

"Look both ways before crossing the street!"

"Hold hands so you don't get lost!"

And finally, that age-old advice upon which Mandi and her family now relied on more than any other: "Go to the nearest adult and report it as soon as you can when you're being bullied."

In fact, Mandi had already tried to practice what all those off-duty officers and well-meaning librarians had been preaching to her all these precious, formative years. On her very first day of school, both she *and* her mother had brought their complaints to the closest adults in charge: The bus driver and his bus monitor.

But not even little Mandi was surprised when her impassioned pleas fell on deaf ears. Everyone and their brother knew it was the teachers who were *really* in charge, and so quietly little Mandi suffered at the hands of her attackers until she made it safely to school.

But as the rush of that first week of first grade swirled by in a blizzard of take-home papers and permission slips, endless announcements and reminders on the intercom, and new faces getting used to new classrooms, few teachers had the time for a single little girl's complaints, let alone on the first day of school. Rebuffed, Mandi told herself she'd wait until the next day to tell her teacher.

When her desk's a little cleaner, she thought.

When there aren't so many announcements nagging her on the intercom.

Where there aren't so many kids huddled around her desk.

When she's turned in the last of the permission slips.

When things calm down.

Tomorrow...

But modern-day elementary schools have a mysterious way of revving up, not slowing down, and Mandi soon found it hard to approach her teacher with her ongoing problems of physical, emotional, and even sexual abuse. Though the Mead boys were still torturing her nonstop before the bus, on the bus, and after the bus, Mandi suffered through the spitting and the punching and the pulling and the shouting and the name calling and the pranks, waiting in vain for just the right time to tell her esteemed first grade teacher, Ms. Arnsbauch*.

But Ms. Arnsbauch was a busy woman, and by the time that long, horrid first week of school was finally and officially over, Mandi had still not come forward and told her teacher about what was really happening to her. Though she'd tried to muster the courage, it just never quite came.

And so she suffered through another torturous bus ride home at the end of that first, fateful week, sprinting straight into her mother's arms when finally she had been delivered to her street. Two whole, torture-free days stretched out luxuriously before her like heaven frosting on marshmallow clouds, and Mandi and her mother breathed a collective sigh of relief.

For her part, Debra felt a similar wave of relief pass over the entire Wein household as Friday afternoon finally arrived and Mandi found herself safe and sound inside the house. It had been a trying week for mother and daughter alike, and neither had slept much at all.

Daily complaints to the bus driver had gone unreported, although Debra hopefully assumed someone, somewhere, would eventually return her calls and ask her help in getting to the bottom of her daughter's problems.

Still, with polite yet quickly straining reserve, she had watched her daughter suffer day after day, only to spend the entire week without a single reply to her almost daily complaints. All the while she hoped that the Mead boys would stop, that the long first week would find them fixated on some other diversion: A cute teacher, a girlfriend, a sport, a hobby, a dead cat.

Who cared, as long as they left poor little Mandi alone.

But the concerned mother's waiting had all been in vain. The attacks continued unabated, and now it was officially too late to do anything about it. Too late to do anything but hold her quivering daughter in her arms and tell her, over and over again, that "everything will be all right. Just wait until Monday, Mandi. Everything will have blown over by then. I promise. It will all go away and this whole, terrible week will seem like a bad dream until finally, one day, you will have forgotten all about it. Just listen to your mother. Have I ever steered you wrong before?"

But even Debra had a hard time believing her own empty promises...

The weekend passed by uneventfully, and far too quickly for both mother *and* daughter. Debra and her father Mark watched fretfully as Mandi stuck close to the house, *too* close, they both thought, with Mandi rarely stepping outside the open front door unless it was with an adult — and even then only briefly.

Mostly the bruised and battered young girl sat quietly in her room, fixated on her favorite dolls and her dog-eared coloring books and whiling away the entire two days off with the familiar surroundings and sounds of her favorite Disney videos. Escaping into a vibrant and colorful world where no one was ever mean to anyone — and even the bad guys came around in the end!

Debra couldn't blame her daughter for wanting to escape into her videos and stuffed animals, but worried fretfully that it wasn't normal for Mandi to not want to go outside and play with the rest of her friends. All summer long, Debra had had a hard time keeping the mischievous young girl *inside* the house — now it seemed as if her daughter was petrified of going *outside*!

Come Sunday night, however, Mandi's peaceful façade finally broke down entirely. The strain of constantly worrying and fretting about the following Monday morning grew too much for the quiet first grader to bear, and just before bedtime she broke down entirely and cried, begging Debra not to "make" her go back to school the next day. Debra's heart broke, for she knew that she could not let little Mandi run away from her problems.

What would *that* teach her?

Instead, she cooed her young daughter to sleep with tender hugs and quiet words, all the while wondering if she were perhaps fooling herself into thinking things would simply work out in the end.

But she and Mark had already talked about it: Better to go through the right channels and not upset the apple cart. Neither parent wanted little Mandi to be labeled a "troublemaker" or "problem child," not in her first week in first grade, after all, and resolved to follow the proper channels to resolve the dispute with those horrible Mead boys on the bus.

Monday morning dawned bright and dreadful for the petrified little girl, who shook and quivered all through an uneaten breakfast. Debra walked Mandi to the bus stop, giving the Mead boys a stern warning about messing with her daughter, but even before she'd made her way back across the street the boys were already crowding poor

Mandi with their threatening posture and coarse language.

Fortunately, the bus arrived soon after and Debra could at least pray that the adults in charge would watch over all of their charges equally, from first graders to sixth. But for little Mandi, watching her familiar street, her house, her front door, and finally her very own mother disappear through the back windows of the bus sounded a death knell inside her breaking little heart.

Immediately, Skeeter yanked Mandi to his seat and reveled in telling her that this was her new "assigned seat." On the crowded bus, with no adult supervision, having already been kicked out of those seats in the front reserved for the "little kids," she had no choice but to believe the bigger, older, tougher boy.

But it wasn't just her seat Mandi had to worry about. Instantly, Skeeter's hands were everywhere: Tousling her hair, pinching her arms, pulling her over to him, sitting her on his rough, coarse lap. The laughter that resulted was deafening; it came from all directions. It seemed the entire bus was reacting to her merciless victimization: From the little kids all the way up front to the big kids way in the back, they were all joining in on the "fun."

Mandi was surrounded by pain and punishment, and she couldn't believe that her weekend was already over. It felt like it had gone by in a flash, and now she was right back where she started, poked and prodded, spat on and shoved, and she hadn't even gotten to school yet!

Quietly, silently, doggedly, Mandi resolved to tell her teacher that very same morning. She had to. She simply couldn't take the abuse any longer. No one could. Why, she was surprised — and not just a little bit proud — that she had endured it all *this* long! But enough was simply enough. She wouldn't — she couldn't — survive the constant, repeated abuse.

Not for another day.

Not for another *two* days.

Surely not for another entire *week*!

But it was like the Mead brothers had a wicked sense of ESP, and their sharp, beady little eyes focused on Mandi with alarming clarity for such devilish grins.

"Don't you dare go squealing to your teacher," they warned her menacingly, their thick shoulders already bunched with muscles, their sinister eyes burning into her very soul. "You think *this* is bad? We can make it all kinds of worse! Just try us. Try telling your teacher, or anyone, and you'll find out. We can make it so bad, you'll wish you'd never been born. We can make it so bad, you'll wish you were *dead*!"

Mandi's tiny heart finished breaking in pieces right then and there. All she'd been taught, all those pat, easy messages that had been all but burned into her brain over the years, were, in the end, worse than useless. No adult could help her, not with ruffians this brutal and devious. They had her cornered, hog-tied, and faced with worst kind of a lose-lose situation: Suffer in silence, and suffer completely, absolutely, dreadfully. Tell an adult, and suffer even *worse*!

But how could it get any worse than it already was!?!

Mandi found out early the next week…

She had suffered in silence long enough, and had finally told Ms. Arnsbauch the awful, horrible truth. But the teacher, who'd always seemed so warm and pleasant to the innocent little first grader, did little to help the situation.

"Are any of the children from the bus in *my* class?" Ms. Arnsbauch asked Mandi in a rare quiet moment.

Mandi looked around the room knowingly, already dreading the answer she would have to give her teacher. Many of the children in her first grade class rode her bus. Many of them whispered behind her back, called her names, and joined in on the daily fun on the bus. But none of them were the Mead brothers, and none of them had ever physically pushed her, or punched her, or spit on her, or worse.

Though she vainly tried to find some loophole in her bewildered first grade mind, in the end Mandi had to confess that, no, none of the boys from the bus were in her first grade class.

"Well then," Ms. Arnsbauch grinned, almost sighing in relief that her culpability was nil. "There's really nothing I can do about it. You'll have to take it up with the principal. Now, if the children were in my class, I could help you. But you said they weren't. So I can't. I'm sorry, Mandi. I really am."

For the first time in her life, Mandi had a hard time believing a grown-up!

Boldly asking for a pass, Mandi was surprised when Ms. Arnsbauch complied. Nervously — Mandi had never seen the inside of the front office before, let alone the principal's office — the little girl walked all the way up the pristine halls of her elementary school and straight into the front office itself.

An efficient and friendly secretary asked Mandi her business, and Mandi replied dutifully: "I'm here to talk to the principal."

"About what?" asked the secretary, her hand already buzzing her boss on the intercom.

But Mandi, perhaps shyly, perhaps defiantly, or more than likely already knowing the futility of her actions, simply demurred and waited until the principal was ready to see her. Principal Marcus Washington* was a tall man, but so are most men to tiny first graders like Mandi Wein.

He listened patiently to Mandi's story, about her nearly two weeks of abuse on the bus, off the bus, in the halls, on the way to class, after class, on the playground, and nodded in all the right spots, even murmuring a sympathetic "I see" or "uhhm hmm," when it seemed appropriate.

Then he went Mandi one better: "I'll get to the bottom of this," said Mr. Washington with a self-satisfied smile. "Those boys won't bother you again."

For perhaps the very first time, Mandi breathed a long, heavy sigh of relief. She had finally been listened to. She had finally been heard. Not just by a bus driver, or a bus monitor. Not just by a teacher, but by the principal himself.

She felt the weight of the world lifted off her shoulders as she fairly skipped back to Ms. Arnsbauch's class, her hall pass damp and sweaty in her nervous little hands. The principal was going to do something about. It was official: That was that.

But as so often happens in the busy and hectic world of an

elementary school bus driver, or bus monitor, or first grade teacher, or even an elementary school principal, life gets in the way of our best intentions.

Mr. Washington never talked to the boys, never called them in, never gave them the "third degree," or even the old principal standby: "the evil eye!"

Nothing was done for little Mandi Wein and her ongoing — and quickly worsening — problem with bullies. Not that day, not the next day, not even the day after that. And so, tragically, another long week of bullying, harassment, and abuse passed by for the hopeful little girl who wanted nothing more than to go to school unmolested and learn what would be taught to her.

Instead she hoped in vain that the principal was a man of his word.

But poor Mandi Wein learned early on what most adults take years to discover: Few men ever are...

FOR THE CHILDREN ...
Putting a Stop to Schoolyard Abuse

HOW TO BE PROACTIVE ABOUT BULLYING:

If your child is being bullied, do something about it! Be proactive toward bullying. If your child tells you that she is being bullied, do something immediately to try to find a solution as quickly as possible. Once again, it is important to communicate with the proper authorities:

An educator at school if the aggression has taken place at school.

A coach or supervisor if you think the aggression has taken place during a sport or leisure activity

The bully's parents or any witness if the aggression has taken place in an unsupervised area (park, street, etc.).

If you need to, don't hesitate to communicate with your local police.

CHAPTER THREE:
Warning Signs

As the very first month of first grade at East Jefferson Elementary School slowly began passing by at an agonizing pace for little Mandi Wein, the rest of the kids in her class settled into their school year and, much to Mandi's dismay, even seemed to *enjoy* themselves tremendously.

Mandi watched enviously as the other little girls in first grade passed by in the halls, carelessly twirling their blond pigtails around their tiny little fingers, popping endless bubbles with their illicit flavors of pink, blue, yellow, green, and even *purple* bubble gum, and generally chittering-chattering each endless day about how *wonderful* first grade was.

Slowly, day by day, hour by hour, Mandi Wein watched helplessly as the gulf widened and divided between herself and the rest of her chipper little first grade class. It amazed her to no end that the other children could actually look forward to school each day, bragging cockily about riding the bus with the "big kids," giggling excitedly about going to lunch, or even groaning out loud when a single minute or two of recess was taken *away* from them!

As for herself, Mandi literally *prayed* for the odd delay or schedule change that would gratefully disrupt the day's routine and thankfully save her a moment or two's torment in the cafeteria or on the playground. A fire drill right before recess was bliss to her. A book fair in the cafeteria sheer heaven: She could eat in the classroom and be safe for one day, at least!

And a bomb scare? Forget about it!

But when book fairs or pranksters couldn't come to her rescue, Mandi found herself asking more and more questions as the time for any activity *outside* of the classroom drew near. Silly, inane questions that made the class squirm in their seats — and drove her teacher mad!

"Could you repeat that last question, ma'am?" Mandi might ask. "I couldn't really hear you over the air conditioning."

Or, "Didn't you say that you were going to grade our papers *before* recess? There's *still* two minutes!"

Or, "Can you hold on just one more second until I find my lunch money? It was right here a second ago..."

Or even, "You said this morning that you were going to penalize us all at recess for Rodney's rude remark. Did you already *forget?*"

She knew it drove everyone crazy, including *herself,* but she just couldn't help it. She would gladly trade the mild discomfort of the rest of her class — or even her frowning teacher — for the few extra minutes of peace and quiet she could enjoy inside the safety of her own first grade classroom.

The rest of the kids just didn't know what it was like...

Mandi knew that she was living in a entirely different world than that of her classmates, a different universe, perhaps, but she simply had no idea how to express to them — or to anyone *else* for that matter — just exactly *what* was happening to her on a daily basis.

Not just about the verbal or physical abuse, the name calling, the curse words, the violence, the implied threats, the sexual harassment, but what was going on *inside* of her. What she was experiencing, in her mind. How her heart was breaking. How her stomach hurt, her head ached constantly, her hands quivered, her eyes teared up at the most inopportune moments.

What she was *feeling...*

Feelings are hard enough for a first grader to explore on her own, let alone vocalize. But to suffer abuse at such a tender age overwhelms the thought processes of any child, especially one suffering the daily onslaught of violence — both real *and* perceived. The stress and grief and fear and pain and unhappiness were growing too much for young Mandi to bear.

It was becoming overwhelming. The dread. The worry. The distress. It ate up all her spare time, like that little chomping yellow ball in that Ms. Pac Man game her mom enjoyed so much at the pizza parlor.

It chewed up her whole day...

The time she should have been twirling her hair around her finger or blowing bubbles with her blue or pink or purple gum or giggling loudly with the other girls was slowly being eaten up by the constant fear.

The daily, grinding fear of being tripped for no reason, or kicked when she wasn't looking, or called another horrible name in front of children she both feared and admired, or pushed down or beat up and picked on or ticked off.

While the other girls worried about homework and extra credit, Mandi worried whether or not someone was going to stick another "Kick Me!" sign on the back of her shirt while she wasn't looking. While the other kids played at recess, Mandi waited for the inevitable confrontation with the bigger kids, hoping against hope that no one would take it too far and hurt her too badly.

This time...

The questions that dogged the other little girls — What will I wear? Does this match? What birthday present should I get my best friend? Is my lunch box cool enough? — were luxuries little Mandi Wein could no longer afford.

Mandi's questions were more akin to those imagined by hardened criminals serving long sentences in prison: Who's got it in for me today? Will I make it through the night? Will I make it through the day? Will tomorrow be the day? When will it come? How will it happen? What can I do?

How will I *survive*?

Though she kept up a brave front for herself, for her teacher, for her principal, for her family, endlessly traipsing off to the bus stop or the cafeteria or the playground each day, a tiny part of Mandi died each time she was called another name, or pushed into another cinder block wall, or spat on, or tripped down the narrow aisle between seats on the bus.

The playful little girl that her parents and sisters had known for nine long years was leaving them, one agonizing moment at a time. It didn't happen overnight, the subtle changes in Mandi's behavior. If they had, perhaps her parents might have been able to realize how agonizing the situation was actually becoming, perhaps her teacher might have stepped in sooner, perhaps her principal might have held up his end of the bargain and actually done his job.

Instead, like an insidious pest that attacks only at the deepest root of the plant, Mandi began changing at her very core, almost infinitesimally, without, perhaps, ever even realizing it herself.

She slept less, tossing and turning and crying out in her sleep where before she had always slept straight through the night, without incident. She became harder to rouse in the morning, and crankier than ever as she slowly woke up to face yet another dreadful day, ever hopeful that things might change, ever disappointed when they inevitably did not.

Her moods grew slowly sour, but not so distasteful that they yet stood out. Most of her erratic behaviors could still be blamed on other, *simpler* things. Her temper was shorter, easier to flare up, but what little girl's isn't? Her appearance grew sloppy, but what little girl's doesn't?

In short, there were a million and one reasons why a little girl might grow moody, sullen, high-strung, irritable, petulant, and angry. A bad grade on a test. A snub by a friend. A harsh look from the teacher.

A bad hair day!

But while Mandi waited for her elementary school principal to help her, while her parents tried the more traditional route of speaking with her teachers and following the school board chain of command, and while the children who tormented her day after day waited with watchful eyes for someone, anyone, to tell them to STOP, the torture continued unabated.

One day, however, it crossed the line…

The day started like any other for Mandi and her family. They said their prayers, crossed their fingers, watched her while she waited at the bus stop without incident, and then hoped and prayed for the next ten to fifteen endless minutes that she would arrive at school safely.

What else could they do?

Mandi *did* arrive safely to school that fateful morning, but not without her fair share of abuse on the bus the whole way there. Instantly drawn into Skeeter's seat by his rough and dirty hands, the abuse and intimidation and scare tactics she'd suffered for these two long weeks started right up again. Mandi squirmed and fought as hard as she could, but there was just no way for her to overpower the much bigger and stronger Mead boy, whose hands seemed to be everywhere — all at once.

He giggled as she writhed, leered as she lunged, and spat as he yelled an endless string of hateful, scathing, stinging epithets while the rest of the bus howled in laughter. Beyond tears, Mandi endured the abuse only by imagining herself in a more pleasant place. A peaceful place.

A *safe* place...

Her bedroom back home, perhaps. Her mother's kitchen, smelling faintly of cinnamon as fall descended on their quiet Rhode Island town and another batch of cookies went from oven to table. Her classroom. A field full of daisies. An evergreen forest. A marshmallow cloud.

"Anywhere but *here*!"

The moments stretched to minutes as the bus made stop after endless stop, each new face symbolizing little more than another audience member for Skeeter and Mandi's non-stop show of ridicule and public humiliation: Same Time, Same Channel!

Occasionally, Mandi would get a temporary reprieve as the lackadaisical bus driver or listless seat monitor issued an obligatory less-than-stern warning: "Cut out that horseplay back there," one of them might grumble. Or "All right now, just calm down, we're almost there."

But instantly, almost as soon as the lone adults on the bus turned their heads or averted their eyes for the briefest of seconds, their ruthless charges just as quickly returned to their torturous pleasures. Finally, the bus squealed to a jerking halt and Mandi fled her seat in tears once more. A momentary glance of the principal as he addressed some students in the commons area caught her eye, lifted her spirits, gave her renewed hope that all might be well, someday, but just as soon a wave of schoolchildren and other teachers swallowed him up and swept him away from the shaking little girl as she stumbled along toward class.

As always, it took Mandi awhile to regain her composure after getting off the bus. Took a while for the trembling to stop, the shaking, the quaking, the churning in her tiny, quivering little guts, the pounding in her head.

Naturally, it took a few minutes for her shoulders to unclench from worrying about who might hit her with a spit wad next. For her trembling fingers to untangle her hair of paper and knots and other things too nauseating to think about.

By then, homeroom was in full swing and one of Mandi's more understanding neighbors had to poke her so that their teacher could take attendance. "Here," Mandi offered her teacher noncommittally, wishing she was anywhere but.

The morning passed, as it always did, in a flutter of activity that was par for the course. From math to reading to social studies, Mandi found it increasingly difficult to concentrate.

If her teacher talked about the cowboys and the Indians, Mandi found herself fantasizing that one or the other would come to her aid and rescue her, skewering Skeeter through his bus seat with a lightning fast arrow or peppering his battered ball cap with musket shot!

If a word problem in math involved trains leaving one station and departing another, Mandi found herself fantasizing what it would be like to hop a train and simply disappear. No more school. No more bus stops. No more "Kick Me!" signs. No more recess. No more spit wads.

No more *Skeeter*...

Halfway through the lesson, Mandi would awake from her reverie to find herself three pages behind the rest of her class, her neighbors giggling at the spacey expression on her face, the faraway glance in her eyes, the pencil just about to fall from her loosened grasp. Then she'd have to literally race through the lesson to catch up with the rest of the class!

Mandi had no idea how she was going to survive first grade — let alone *pass* it!

Finally, the time the rest of the class waited for arrived with a fluttering of sweaters and tightening of shoelaces: recess! The girls and boys who shared her classroom with her every day squealed and giggled as they streamed through the back door and out onto the playground.

As always, Mandi dawdled slowly behind her classmates, dragging her feet across the classroom floor and blinking at the bright sunlight while her teacher, Ms. Arnsbauch, sighed and scuttled her right out the door.

"Honestly, Mandi," said her teacher. "It's like you don't even *want* to go outside and play!"

How Mandi would have given anything if her teacher would have only asked her, "Why?" Instead it was off to the teacher's lounge, or perhaps up to the front office, or maybe even off campus to the bank to deposit her weekly paycheck. Leaving Mandi to the devious devices of a playground full of ruffians and scoundrels who would do her harm the first chance they got.

It didn't take long...

Mandi might have been all right had her recess period been filled with only first graders, or perhaps even first and second graders mixed together. That she could have handled. That she could have survived. But in the fits and starts of back-to-school scheduling, there were only so many recess periods available each day, and they had to shared by the whole school — six entire grade levels.

Thus second graders often shared the monkey bars with fourth graders, and sixth graders often played kickball with third graders.

Here and there a stray teacher chirped into her cell phone or scanned the morning paper with her bifocals, while two or three more stood nearby in a clump watching the children with one eye and their watches with the other, preening their faces upward for a stray ray of sunlight or sipping on a diet soda for a quick burst of energy to finish out the day.

Invariably, from ninety to one hundred and twenty to upwards of two *hundred* children prowled the monkey bars and see saws, the slides and swings, the sand lot and bleachers.

While teachers saw little more than a peacefully milling crowd of happy children, some running, some laughing, some shouting, some sitting, the merciless caste society that is a modern American elementary school playground reigned supreme — and with an iron fist!

Like a better-dressed version of *Lord of the Flies*, only the strong survived — and took it out on the weak! Depending on the time of day and the whims of schoolyard scheduling, it might have been the fourth graders ruling the roost at 10 a.m., or the sixth graders running roughshod over the rest of the school at noon.

Meanwhile, kids like Mandi hunkered down as best they could, staying close to the teachers on "recess duty," avoiding the kids in the upper grades, and never, *ever* dipping out of sight for too long.

But on this day, on this *one* day at least, little Mandi Wein finally let down her guard. For only the briefest of moments, Mandi let herself be a kid again. For a split second too long, or perhaps even a fraction of that time, Mandi ignored her fears and indulged herself in a simple recess diversion. Becoming absorbed in her game of tic-tac-toe in the sand, or perhaps her jacks, Mandi spent one moment too many looking down when she should have been looking up.

In that mere moment, that tiny instant, the teacher who'd been standing nearby moved to another corner of the sidewalk and the hawks, the *vultures*, who were on constant "Mandi vigil" alerted the powers that be.

Like the blood-sucking insect from which his nickname derived, Skeeter swooped in and surrounded Mandi in the teacher's sudden absence. By the time she looked up from her innocent child's play, from the time she put back up the guard that had become her constant companion, it was far too late. Only this time Mandi had more to fear from Skeeter and his friends than spit wads and curse words.

This time, Skeeter had a pencil.

A *sharp* one...

"Ouch," cried Mandi as her bigger, older, smarter, meaner tormentor began poking her with the stiff and pointy #2 pencil. "You're not supposed to be over here. Leave me alone or I'll tell!"

"Who?" asked Skeeter mercilessly, almost gloating, sticking her in the shoulder, the ankle, mussing up her hair with the pencil, enjoying his recess more than ever. "Who are you going to tell, Mandi? Huh? Huh? None of the teachers are here to save you this time. You're all alone."

Mandi quivered, looking left, looking right, seeing for herself that Skeeter was telling the truth. Picking up on the little girl's fear, feeding off of it, Skeeter prodded more insistently with the sharpened writing utensil, poking Mandi's chest, her abdomen, and finally plunging the pencil into the crotch of her pants with a triumphant look on his leering face.

"Gotcha," said the look. "Gotcha right where it counts!"

Finally, feeling the sting of pencil lead on the soft flesh of her vulnerable inner thigh, Mandi screamed out, scattering her tormentors to the far ends of the recess yard and finally, mercifully, drawing the attention of a nearby teacher. Seeing the blood on her inner thigh and even the mark left behind by the pencil lead, the teacher notified Ms. Arnsbauch, and Mandi was allowed to go to the school nurse, who patched up the cut and did her best to soothe the young girl's nerves as well.

Mandi, perhaps sensing a blessing in disguise and hoping that the boys had finally hit rock bottom and might now be reprimanded, told everyone she could about the incident: the teacher on the playground, her own teacher, Ms. Arnsbauch, the school nurse, the principal's secretary, even the principal himself.

Unfortunately this incident, no matter how much more severe it had been than the others, would have exactly the same result: none.

It was 11 a.m. in the morning and Mandi's tormentors had finally crossed the threshold from threats to action. Encouraged by the mob, fueled by the freedom of under-vigilant teachers and overcrowded playgrounds, all but encouraged by a prevalent lack of discipline and overall absence of any supervision, Mandi's tormentors had rounded the bend from intimidation and reverted to outright violence.

All before noon...

The school nurse called Mandi's mother, Debra Wein, at 3:45 that afternoon. Understandably, Debra was a little more than upset. After hearing the lurid and violent details of the offense and noting that the school had waited almost five solid hours to notify her, she called the principal as soon as she got off with the nurse. Once she got Mr. Washington on the phone, she railed at him about the offense and asked him if he was finally ready to do something, *anything*, about it.

His reply was as unsatisfactory as it was brief, "I'm sorry," he said noncommittally. "This kind of thing has never happened before. Why, pencils aren't even allowed on the recess yard."

Either are spit wads or bubble gum or 'Kick Me' signs or staples or rubber bands, Debra thought to herself ruefully. *Yet Mandi's been assaulted by all of those on the recess yard as well!*

Principal Washington told Debra that the boys' parents would be notified, yet after being brushed off before by the faculty and administration at East Jefferson Elementary School, she instinctively pressed for more. A meeting at the school. Both parents of the children there. Principal Washington serving as an intermediary. An open forum where the problem could be discussed, hashed out, argued about if necessary, but ultimately resolved.

At least this time Principal Washington got wise and didn't make the same mistake twice: He offered Debra no promises this time. After days of waiting and numerous phone calls, Debra noted that the boys' parents were never called and no disciplinary action was ever taken as a result of the physical assault on her daughter during recess that fateful day.

Another opportunity missed.

Another signal sent.

A signal that said, loud and clear: You can do just about anything at East Jefferson Elementary School and get away with it...

FOR THE CHILDREN ...
Putting a Stop to Schoolyard Abuse

WHAT TO TELL YOUR CHILD IF SHE IS BEING BULLIED:

One of your first steps in helping your child cope with bullying is bolstering their self-esteem. To do that, here are some things to tell a child if you believe that he or she is being bullied:

That she has the right **not** to be bullied.

That it is not her fault if she is bullied.

That she should not have to face this on her own and that she can confide in you.

That she should not try to tackle bullies on her own.

CHAPTER FOUR:
How Can It Go On?

There are moments in a mother's life when her vision suddenly crystallizes, when time stands still, and when a situation becomes all-too-clear. When the hype and the hope and the wishing and the dreaming and the fooling oneself dissolves like a bitter shot of Alka-Seltzer. When, as if an auto-zoom focus has been placed directly in front of her, her life suddenly comes into crystal clear focus.

When, once and for all, she finally stops fooling herself. . .

When she stops thinking that things will "just get better." When she starts seeing the forest for the trees. When she stops relying on others to do what she knows she must do for herself.

When the minutes and the hours and the weeks and the endless days and the sleepless nights spent frowning and fretting and hoping it would all just go away become useless, and reality smacks her dead in the middle of her face with a brisk "I told you so" that leaves her reeling in its wake.

For Debra Wein, that moment came while speaking, yet again, to her daughter's principal at East Jefferson Elementary School...

As so often happens, that fateful day had started out like any other: With the constant battle to rouse a drowsy and unwilling Mandi from her bed and get her ready for another dreadful day of school. With the frenzied dash to make a hot, hearty breakfast and feed three daughters, not to mention a hungry husband. With the smiles, the laughs, the frowns, the fights of a modern, American family in the throes of work and home and school and family and love and life and another normal day just trying to keep their heads above water.

Understandably, Mandi whined about heading off to the bus stop when it was finally time for her to leave the safety of her warm, cozy, familiar kitchen. Debra understood. Probably more than her simpering daughter would every really hope to understand.

Her heart ached for poor Mandi, ached with a pain that only a concerned mother could every truly understand, but with an overriding knowledge that didn't quite allow her to give herself over to those sympathetic feelings. Debra Wein knew, in her deepest heart of hearts, breaking though it was, that they were never going to get over this hump if life in their household couldn't proceed normally.

If Debra couldn't be a normal mother.

If Mandi couldn't be a normal daughter.

If she couldn't rely on the fact that her daughter could be safe from physical and sexual abuse at her very own bus stop!

The Weins had already been assured by the principal, Mr. Washington, that Mandi would be safe, both *on* school grounds — and off. The frazzled mother of three growing daughters had to go on that, had to trust that, had to *believe* that.

After all, this was a professional man, an educated man, a salaried man whose very job relied on the success of his performance on a daily basis. How could a man like that possibly ever let an innocent little first grader be assaulted, day after day after *day*, at her bus stop of all places?

He wouldn't.

He *couldn't*...

Debra tried to convince her middle daughter that things would be okay, that today would be different, that those horrible Mead brothers would leave her alone — for once. It was hard to physically say the words, to get them out of her trembling mouth, particularly when she wasn't quite sure if she believed them herself. But she had to be strong for her daughter. For her family.

For *herself*...

Eventually Mandi grabbed her cheery lunch box full of all of her favorite comfort foods and tentatively, hesitantly headed for the family's front door. Debra's heart nearly broke to see the little girl's hand trembling ever so slightly as she bravely turned the doorknob, but she forced herself, *willed* herself to be strong as Mandi headed out the door without so much as a glance over her shoulder.

Debra promised herself she would watch the bus stop, look out for Mandi, make sure those Mead brothers weren't at it again. And she did. At first. She watched Mandi walk down the stairs, waved to her as she looked both ways before crossing the street, and frowned as she dragged her feet to the local bus stop to await an uncertain and tenuous fate.

But after a few precious minutes without violence, without abuse, without cursing, without physical attack, Debra heard the daily grind of a busy morning calling to her from the chaotic mess left behind by her loving family.

The dishes to do. The kitchen to clean. The chores to attack. The ringing phone. The blaring television. The gurgling coffee pot. She could still keep a watch out for Mandi until the bus came, she told herself. She could still keep one eye on Mandi, and another on the house.

Couldn't she?

But in the blistering pace of elementary school physics, all it takes is a split second to ruin someone's morning, not to mention their entire day. Their very *life*. To shout out an unforgivably brutal name, a curse word, a nasty epithet. To trip, to punch, to maim, to push. To bully, to bluster, to bruise. One washed dish, one ring of the phone, one glance away, can mean a lifetime to a frightened little girl who is momentarily powerless at the hands of her older tormentors.

For her part, Mandi approached the bus stop that morning with her usual sense of fear and trepidation. She tried to follow her mother's lead and be strong, tried to be happy and smiling like her two loving sisters, tried to absorb her father's inherent strength and courage.

She tried so very, very hard…

But the walk to the bus stop each morning became more and more like a death knell, an execution, a burial of her childish hopes and dreams. It started as soon as she stepped foot on the hallowed ground of her bus stop. All noise ceased. All activity stopped. The kids were expecting her.

No, they were *waiting* for her...

They lurked in gaggles and gangs, great gooey globs of bored and restless schoolchildren giggling behind their fingers — and pointing behind her back. Sometimes the violence erupted immediately, all of a sudden, out of the blue, two or three of the older boys surrounding her the minute she showed up and tormenting her continuously until the bus arrived.

Other times she was lulled into temporary complacency, thinking she might be okay. Thinking that this time, just this once, oh please let it be, they might ignore her and simply let her be!

One minute, then two, then three, then perhaps *five* blissful minutes would tick by mercilessly, while nothing happened. Not one thing. The birds would chirp. The cars would pass. The dew would drop. Then all of a sudden the world would collapse around her as fists and feet and tongues lashed out at her with a flurry of volleys, names, curse words, violence.

She never knew when it would come, how it would come, why it would come, or who it would come from. Certainly, the Mead brothers instigated most of it. But they were not alone. If one of them were absent, or thankfully even all three, and she thought she had it made, some younger punk, an underclassmen, might take over where they left off the day before.

Mandi felt like a rusty, dented baton being passed back and forth in some insidious game of tag that never, *ever* ended. Sometimes it took three kids to bring her to tears, other times it only took one. Sometimes it would be the boys ganging up on her, other times it would just be the girls. Sometimes, like the polar opposite of her favorite super heroes, both groups might join forces in the fight against Mandi's safety and well-being.

This day, this cruel, fateful day, it would be a combination of all of the above...

It started with the names. Someone called Mandi fat. That she could take. That wouldn't make her cry. She'd heard that before. But then more words flew. Faster and faster. So fast she didn't know how to respond, didn't know what to say, didn't know how to react. Many of the words were so brutal, so foreign, she didn't even know what they meant!

But her hesitation, her indecision, her paralysis only seemed to feed the anger of the other children. Their voices grew louder, their taunts more insistent, their epithets more insulting as they drew closer and closer, spittle accompanying their venom as Mandi stood in their midst, powerless.

"You fat bitch," they shouted.

"You little slut," they called.

"Whore."

"Tramp."

"Fat-ass!"

"RETARD!"

It was the venomous vocabulary known only to American public schools — and perhaps prisons. An escalating diatribe born of ignorance and immaturity, anger and fear. Words heard on TV, in the movies, at the dinner table while the children's parents fought over another overdue credit card bill or missed mortgage payment.

Faster and faster came the words, closer and closer encroached the crowd. Mandi could feel the impending violence in the air, crackling like lightning on the near horizon. It came from every angle: in front, behind, to the right, to the left. Big, tall, short, fat, first grade, third grade, sixth grade.

Though she had expected it, the first push caught her by surprise. But the second didn't. Nor did the third. It was escalating, and though Mandi didn't know the word, she knew the feeling. Getting worse. Louder. Stronger. Rougher. Meaner.

How could the bus not be here yet?

How could no one stop this?

Why were they doing it?

What had she done to deserve this?!?

But no one was there to answer Mandi's questions as the ravenous crowd descended upon her, kicking, pushing, shoving, squealing, screaming, pulling, yelling, shouting, cursing, spitting.

The growing crowd fenced her in, surrounded her, taking on a life of its own, a mindless consciousness. It subtly moved her exactly where it wanted her to go, pushing her this way, farther from home, toward the street, away from the safety of her mother's arms, her kitchen window, her front door.

She desperately tried to break free, finally succumbing to the tears that had threatened all morning. Suddenly, satisfied, the crowd parted momentarily. It was the moment they'd been waiting for, the payoff, the climax.

"It took a little longer this morning," Mandi could imagine the boys bragging to their friends during homeroom. "But we made that bitch cry after all!"

Instinctively, the brave little girl surged through the crowd and dashed for home. She sprinted on wobbly knees, certain she would fall and smash her face in, scrape her scalp to the bone, ruin her still-new school clothes. She was shaking, trembling, quaking all the way.

Somehow she made it up the endless stairs, bursting through the door crumpled and rumpled and overwrought. There was no other word to describe her but overwrought. Her mother sensed it immediately, wrapped her into her arms, held her tight, crying herself for the insanity of it all. The brutality.

The injustice…

But she couldn't let Mandi give in, give up. Together they marched down the stairs and across the street and straight up to the bus stop. Debra said not a word, nor did her daughter, but the message was clear: No more.

Together the two Wein women stood trembling amongst the heartless little children who daily tormented Mandi, waiting impatiently for the bus to come and deliver the little girl from her daily abuse. When it did, Debra put her on the bus herself and insisted that she sit in the front of the bus, little kids or no.

First grade isn't little enough? she thought to herself as the bus monitor grudgingly acquiesced to her heated demands.

Alone now, still trembling, Debra watched the familiar yellow bus lurch away from the corner and whisk her little daughter off to school. Before it was even out of sight, she found herself back across the street and dialing the by-now familiar number of East Jefferson Elementary School.

Debra barely waited for a greeting when the ringing ended and the school secretary answered the phone. "Get me the principal," she said immediately, innately trying to gather her thoughts so she wouldn't come off as just another irrational mother trying to protect her little baby.

Debra could tell by his tone that the principal was not eager to hear from her, especially not at such an early hour. But neither did she care: It wasn't too early in the morning for her poor daughter to be physically and verbally abused at *his* bus stop. It certainly wasn't too early to call the man and complain about it!

In short order, the concerned mother explained what had happened to her daughter that morning at the bus stop. That should have been enough to goad any principal worth his salt into action. But despite her attempts to remain calm, Debra launched into a chronology of events that began with the very same kinds of behavior perpetrated against her daughter on the first day of school!

The threats, the taunts, the innuendo, the seating on the bus, the kicking, the pushing, the shoving, the cursing, the teasing, the molesting, the anger, the violence, the overwhelming atmosphere of permissiveness and lack of discipline that allowed the unwarranted abuse to continue, day after day.

Even before she was finished, she had the sense that Mr. Washington was itching to interrupt her. Spent, Debra listened to the principal make excuses for those daily instigators of her daughter's abuse: the Mead brothers.

"I understand your concern," he said, or something to that effect. "But I caution to remind you that the boys themselves are having a rough life. They are being raised by a single father, and aren't doing too well in school."

Debra assured her daughter's principal that she meant the boys no harm, and as a mother even wished them well in their family strife, but she argued that their rough home life shouldn't translate into an unacceptable abuse of her daughter! "I'm sorry," she said, firmly. "But I can't see as how that's any of my concern. I understand their problems, but that's no excuse. I'm concerned first and foremost with my daughter, not the home life of the boys who are tormenting her! Something has to be done."

"I'll speak with the father," said Principal Washington, effectively ending the discussion of not only her daughter's problems, but her safety as well.

Debra hung up the phone, staring at it plaintively as the reality of her situation became suddenly as clear as crystal: She was alone. That was painfully clear to her by now. No knight in shining armor was going to come and rescue her. No school principal was going to solve her daughter's problem.

After all, a man who cast off personal responsibility for repeated physical and verbal abuse by blaming it all on a "poor home life" was obviously too concerned about protecting his own interests, than worrying about the safety of her daughter. It was the classic academic excuse for anything that went wrong in the real world. But her daughter's pain was too severe, too real, to be blamed on simple upbringing.

And Debra wasn't into making excuses.

Not for her own children, or anyone else's, for that matter...

No, Debra could hear the words practically shouting between the lines of Mr. Washington's well-clipped phrases and "school speak." In all likelihood it was quite possible that he *would* talk to the father of the Mead boys. But talk was cheap, and besides, what was a single father going to do about it? He already obviously couldn't control his boys as it was.

What was a pat speech from their principal going to do about it?

Besides, Debra had seen up close the anger in those boys' eyes. Had seen the fear and rage practically boiling from their skin as she'd stood guard over Mandi at the bus stop. The out and out anger seething behind those beady little eyes was not going away simply because of a pep talk.

Barring several sessions with a trained therapist, only severe penalties were going to change the actions of the Mead brothers, and she'd heard no concrete plans to do anything to them when she'd spoken with the harried principal. No detentions, no suspensions, no home visits, not even a half-hearted essay entitled "We will not torture Mandi Wein at the bus stop anymore!"

No, the Weins were on their own. It was as plain to Debra Wein as the nose on her face, or the quivering fear in her little daughter's eyes. It would be up to her to lend Mandi strength to go to school every day. It would be up to her father to lend a supportive shoulder to cry on, a strong hand to hold. It would be up to her daughters to give their sister some much-needed tender loving care.

With the school unable — or unwilling — to remedy the situation, it was up to the Weins to weather the storm themselves. Surely, between keeping a close eye on the bus stop and keeping up the pressure on Mandi's counselor, teacher, and principal, the abuse would end. Surely, the boys would tire of making Mandi cry and move on to other children.

Other victims...

But the Weins were in for a surprise — perhaps even the biggest surprise of their life — as that fall quietly ended and December yawned its way into their collective calendars. The abuse continued. Day after day, week after week, month after month. It was insidious, calculated, and prolific. It never slowed down, never sped up, never quite stopped, never quite got so bad that any bones were broken or noses were bloodied or skirts were torn or blouses ripped off.

But it ground on, every single day. With Mandi, and the rest of the devoted Wein family, helpless to do a single thing about it. They watched, they lurked, they called, they wrote, they confronted, they called some more. None of it worked. Not the honey, not the vinegar. Not the pleading, not the threats.

In reality, the forces they were dealing with were too great to overcome. The Mead brothers, and their countless accomplices, proved too great to vanquish. When the Weins slept fitfully, the children plotted mercilessly. Where adult sensibilities prevailed, they had no sway over the modern mentality of a school full of bullies. Where conscience erred, injustice flourished...

Mandi suffered cruelly at the hands of her tormentors, but even she got used to the daily, weekly, monthly patterns of abuse. From bus stop to recess to the cafeteria and back to the bus stop, it swirled around her like a swarm of bees she simply for the life of her just could not shake.

Some days it was the name calling. Other days it was the pushing. Most days it was both. Shoving often gave way to kicking, kicking often gave way to threats, always the bullies kept at it until Mandi was quivering mass before them. Reduced to tears, trembling with emotions and stress she simply couldn't cope with, Mandi continued her almost daily complaints to the "grown-ups" at school.

The teachers.

The counselors.

Her principal.

All in vain. Winter passed to spring and soon summer showed up, and with it the promise of ten unspoiled weeks of safety, freedom, and restful nights. No one looked forward to June, July, and August that year more than little Mandi Wein.

And yet her family was overwhelmed by the change in their middle daughter. Where once Mandi had frolicked outside with the other children, now she seemed petrified to leave the house — unless she was accompanied by her mother or father. And even that wasn't a guarantee that the young girl would feel safe.

Trips to the mall found the shell-shocked youngster exhausted from constantly being on the lookout for some kid from school who might immediately begin the name calling, taunting, and teasing that had marked her every school day. Going to the grocery store, the movies, the park proved no less traumatic for the tiny little girl who all but walked on eggshells every time she left the house.

Mark and Debra thought surely as the summer days rolled by that their daughter would finally unwind, relax, calm down. That her nightmares would end, her agoraphobia improve, her mood lighten.

But it never did...

As so often happens, summer ended almost as soon as it began. The restful nights, the family dinners, the sleepy mornings, the pancake breakfasts, the water balloon fights, far too soon they all came to an abrupt and unwilling end.

Suddenly, it was time for back-to-school shopping.

Suddenly, it was time for alarm clocks to be set.

Suddenly, it was time for the Wein girls to go to bed early.

Suddenly, it was time...for second grade!

FOR THE CHILDREN ...
Putting a Stop to Schoolyard Abuse

WHAT TO DO IF YOUR CHILD IS BEING BULLIED:

What should your child do if she is being bullied? The answer is not clear cut, as every case of bullying, just like every other crime, is unique to both the bully and his victim. However, here are a few guidelines to help your child when and if she is bullied on school grounds:

Your child must remain calm and not act scared. She should try not to show that she is upset or angry because bullies love to get a reaction. If your child stays calm and hides her emotions, bullies might get bored and leave her alone.

Your child should answer bullies firmly in short sentences such as, "Yes. No. Leave me alone." She mustn't start a discussion or argue with bullies to provoke them.

Remember to tell your child that violence never solves anything. Your child must avoid fighting. Should she feel threatened, she should give the bullies what they want. Remind her that personal property is not worth an injury.

Your child must then observe the bullies carefully and remember as much information as possible: height, age, hair color, clothes, etc.

CHAPTER FIVE:
Second Grade

As incredible as it sounds, almost from the very moment, from the very minute, that Mandi Wein walked onto the bus stop on the first day of second grade, the torment began.

Again...

It was like a nightmare that little Mandi could not escape. While it seemed the rest of the kids at the bus stop had mushroomed over the summer, Mandi herself looked almost exactly the same. Sure, she was a year older, a year wiser, a year smarter, but everyone else seemed to have eclipsed her in maturity and "street smarts."

From the very moment she left the house that morning the first day of school, Mandi had to almost convince herself that things would be better, things would be different, things would be sane!

She hardly slept the night before, alternately dreading the following day and allowing herself to naively believe that she could invisibly walk through an entire school year without running for cover every time the Mead brothers showed up on the scene.

They showed up almost immediately, and indeed it seemed to Mandi as if the boys had been waiting all summer for her to show up so that they could have some fun. Especially Skeeter! How could they have not grown up by now? How could they have not gotten bored with Mandi?

More importantly, how could they have never, ever, once gotten into trouble for all they had put Mandi through during first grade?!?

In a way, although certainly not while they were tormenting her, but in a way Mandi couldn't even blame the Mead boys. After all, they were simpletons, to be sure. Cretins with no home life, no mother, a father who could care less. Why wouldn't they be bad? Why wouldn't they be creeps? Why wouldn't they pick on a poor, innocent, little, defenseless first grader to torment?

It made perfect sense: Older kids might fight back. Tougher kids certainly would. Bigger kids wouldn't stand for it. Smarter kids would find a way to squeal to the high heavens and never be bothered again. And rich kids?

Rich kids would have threatened Principal Washington before the first week was out. But little Mandi was a normal girl from a normal family. Like the rest of us, she assumed that justice would be done, simply because that was the right thing to do about it. That the Mead boys would just grow up. That Principal Washington would come to his senses and suspend the boys, or worse, expel them. That he would send some kind of message.

But, again, she couldn't blame the Mead boys. They were ruffians, tough boys, and respected only authority. Obviously, the message had been sent early on in first grade: Mandi Wein is fair game. Mandi Wein is fresh meat. Mandi Wein is free for the taking.

Scream at her. Yell at her. Kick her. Beat her. Punch her. Spit on her. Call her names. Curse. Fight. Do whatever it is you want to her, because the word is out: Principal Washington doesn't care. The counselors don't care. The teachers don't care. They hear Mandi coming, they roll their eyes and brace themselves for some new complaint, some new offense, some new threat.

And all the while the children watched. Watched closely the reactions of the adults. When the teachers blew Mandi off, they knew the halls and playgrounds and cafeteria were safe to torment Mandi. When the bus drivers blew Mandi off, they knew the bus stop, and both trips back and forth to school were "pick on Mandi" times. When the counselors blew Mandi off, they knew that no one would ever take her seriously ever again.

And when Principal Washington blew her off? When their own principal ignored the threats, slapped them on the wrist, never even called in their father, never even gave them detention, never even suspended them? That was when they knew the whole school was one big playground for their murderous intent.

All summer they had probably been brewing new plots for little Mandi. All summer they had probably laughed about the abuse they had dished out on the poor little first grader: Remember that time we made her eat sand at the bus stop? What about that "kick me" sign? No, wait. Remember that time at recess? That was the best! How many times did you make her cry? What about you? I can beat that...

They were probably itching to get back to school, if only to pick up picking on Mandi right where they had left off. They had probably planned it, for months and weeks and surely nights on end: First, we can do this. Then, we can do that. What about this? What about that? Oh, that's a good one. Wait'll we do this! Or that. Or this!

And, just like that, second grade was here. Mandi walked to the bus stop, waved to her mother, watched her close the front door, and quivered and quaked as the torment continued. Skeeter and Pugsley descended on her like vultures over fresh road kill, sniffing out her fear, her immaturity, her trust, her faithfulness in the system, her truth and honesty, exploiting it with their ingenuity and spite.

The names were first. Worse ones this year, as if she had graduated from first grade to second grad and now the gloves were finally off: They could call her anything they ever wanted to, and then some! Names Mandi had never heard before, but was surely to hear every day — every singe day — for the rest of the school year spilled from the mouths of Mandi's fellow schoolchildren as if they'd been stored up for three long months.

"Bitch!"

"Whore!"

"Fat pig!"

"Fat ____-ing pig!"

"Slut!"

"____-ing slut!"

Oh, how she longed to be back in her bed, safe under the covers, listening to her sisters snore and whimper as the dawn crept slowly above the windowsill. Oh, how she wished she could be anywhere,

anywhere, but at this bus stop with these idiots and their violence, profanity, and hate.

And even when the bus arrived, there was no relief. Not for a second. The same old bus driver. The same old bus monitor. The same seats. "Little kids only up front, no exceptions!"

And there went Mandi, shuffled to the middle of the bus by a crowd of older hooligans, just out of sight of the big rearview mirror. Just under the radar of the adults on board. Mercilessly poked and prodded and accosted and abused. Over and over and over again.

Only to wind up at school, where a disbelieving adult — who had no doubt heard the rumors about little Mandi — would listen patiently.

And do nothing...

Where the counselor would roll their eyes.

And do nothing...

Where Principal Washington himself would listen to little Mandi, pat her on her head, nod sympathetically, frown disapprovingly, perhaps even jot down a name or two, send her on her way.

And do nothing...

Mandi somehow made it through that first day back and literally dropped into her mother's arms the minute she got back home. And then, only then, did the stories pour out of her quivering little chest. As fast as she could relate them.

"And then, Skeeter did this..."

"And then, Pugsley said that..."

"There's a new kid. Even he started in on me!"

"Mommy, what does this word mean?"

"What about that one?"

For her part, Debra could not believe her ears. Nor could she reconcile her deep disappointment with the administration down at East Jefferson Elementary school. After all, she too had spent a fitful night hoping, praying, fervently begging that this year, that second grade, might change the way Mandi was treated at school.

She had racked her brain, over and over again, tossing and turning into the wee hours of the morning, hoping for a solution if they didn't.

What could she do differently this year? How could she respond better to Mandi's complaints? How could she force the principal to listen to her? How could she take things to the next level?

And, hoping against hope that she wouldn't have to…

But here was Mandi, four in the afternoon on the first day back to school and already in tears. And how many days were left? 179? Days and weeks and months? Halloween and Thanksgiving and Christmas and New Year's and Valentine's Day and on and on? How could this go on? How could this continue?

How could this be happening *all over again*?

The answer was as simple as the nose on her face: It *couldn't*!

Immediately, without even hesitating, Debra called Principal Washington at the school. Explaining that she had hoped second grade would not be a repeat of first, Debra explained what had happened at the bus stop, once Mandi got to school, and on the bus the whole way home.

Even as the horrible words spilled from her lips, she felt as if she had stepped into a time machine and was repeating the entire previous year all over again. Even Principal Washington's pat response — "I assure you, Mrs. Wein, that I'll talk to those boys and put a stop to this" — sounded word for word like the empty promises he had made a year earlier.

But even if those nasty Mead brothers — and even her daughter's principal — hadn't changed over the summer, one thing was for sure: Debra had! She had watched her little girl go from a hopeful, confused, trusting, loyal, obedient first grader to a bewildered, frightened, distrustful, emotional second grader.

And she wasn't going to put up with it. Not again, she wasn't.

Not this year.

Not *ever*!

From that very moment, from that first day of school forward, Debra made a concerted effort to call the school almost every single day of Mandi's tenure as a second grader at East Jefferson Elementary School. Day after day, week after week, month after month, Debra would call with specific incidents, complaints, reports, abuse. She knew every intimate detail of Mandi's abuse.

She knew every curse word, every "Kick Me" sign, every epithet, innuendo, and humiliation her daughter endured. Even when Mandi didn't even realize she was being abused, Debra recognized the signs. And she reported every single one!

The secretaries at Mandi's school soon grew to recognize her voice — even the "temps" who were only there for a few short days at a time could tell when it was Debra on the phone! Principal Washington certainly knew every intonation of Debra's voice. From the anger to the betrayal to the hurt to the sincerity to the outrage.

Yet while he couldn't ignore her repeated complaints about her daughter's welfare, the principal of her daughter's school did little — perhaps even *less* than that, if it was at all humanly possible — to rectify the situation. The abuse continued unabated. Monday. Tuesday. Wednesday. Thursday. Friday.

The days of the school week all blurred together into one homogenized blend of suffrage and abuse. Yet this was not some third-world country, not some communist state. This was America. This was Rhode Island. This was a public school! Staffed by so-called professionals, who were paid for by her tax dollars, and there to provide both education — and safety — for Mandi and children just like Mandi.

And yet here they were, a year after her daughter had been verbally, mentally, physically, and even sexually abused, and nothing. Not an apology. Not a phone call. Not a conference. Not a suspension. Not an expulsion.

Not even a detention…

Still, even with the mounting evidence that neglect was taking place, Debra tried in vain to put herself into the principal's shoes. She knew he had a big responsibility. Knew he had 700 other children to worry about. Knew he only had so many hours in the day and so many other problems to deal with: absentee students, truancy, tardiness, burned out teachers, lack of funds, the whole modern public school ball of wax.

And all of it riding squarely on his shoulders…

But there were bigger schools across the nation where abuse didn't take place. Where first graders were coveted, respected, and best of all, protected. Where mothers didn't have to tell their first graders what "whore" or "slut" or "tramp" meant. Where daughters didn't have bags under their eyes from lack of sleep. Where the mere sign of a school bus didn't send shivers down the students' spines!

Debra knew that she wasn't asking a lot. Heck, she sometimes thought she wasn't even asking enough. After all, was it too much to ask for her daughter to be safe? Too much to ask for her daughter to go one single, solitary school day without breaking into tears?

By lunch time?

Yet still, no matter what tactic she tried, Debra watched helplessly as her second grade daughter dragged herself off to school each day for another round of assault. Without recourse. Without relief.

Without justice...

Amazingly, through it all, Mandi continued to have a social life in the brief, stolen minutes she had in the safety and security of her own second grade classroom. Though she dreaded the bus stop, the bus ride, recess, PE, and lunch time, Mandi could flourish inside the classroom, where for some reason, away from the mob mentality of the "big kids," her second grade peers apparently accepted her for the charming little girl she could be.

In this sanctuary, Mandi could color, read, learn, concentrate, and hope for a brighter future than the reality of her day-to-day existence. Though she could not control life outside the classroom walls, Mandi could decide for herself how to behave in Mrs. Simpson's* second grade class.

She could choose to turn in her work on time. Choose to read silently or out loud. Choose her friends, her math buddies, do her homework, color in the lines, and do anything and everything other normal little second graders do.

It was only outside of her classroom where hell reigned and fire burned...

But inside, Mandi even managed to find a little friend. A companion with which to share her hopes, her dreams, her desires, her fears — and even the occasional colored pencil or crayon!

Millie Gurber* got along swimmingly with little Mandi Wein. The two swapped desserts at lunch, graded each other's papers when asked to do so, and through Millie's loyal friendship Mandi was finally able to see "how the other half lived!"

She could pretend, at least for a few short hours a day, that she wasn't the school's whipping post. That she wouldn't get kicked or pushed or shoved or spat on or cursed that day after school. That she wouldn't be harassed, threatened, or molested the next morning at the bus stop.

That she wasn't trapped in a living hell...

Millie and Mandi. Mandi and Millie. Debra could finally breathe a sigh of relief: Mandi had something, someone, to divert her thoughts and give her hope. To take her away from the misery of the bus stop and recess and the cafeteria, and bring her courage to face the rest of her day.

And so it was with much sadness and alarm that Debra opened the front door one day after school to find Mandi crying. Not that this was an unusual event: Mandi cried, on average, well, every day after school. But today's thunderstorm of crocodile tears and quivering shoulders and trembling hands were particularly vehement, and it was several long minutes before Mandi finally told her what had happened.

Mandi revealed that early that very morning Millie had broken the bad news to Mandi with the following words: "I can't be your friend because you're Jewish and my mother hates Jews. You need to get Jesus in your life!"

Naturally, Debra was appalled. *What next?* she thought to herself exasperatedly as she picked up the phone yet again in preparation for another afternoon phone call to Principal Washington. *What is going on down at that school? Are we in the Twilight Zone? Am I trapped in Nazi Germany?!?*

Of course, Mandi's principal agreed to "talk to the girl," which did little good. In addition to being the school whipping post, Mandi was now the classroom outcast, and Millie's very vocal religious belief — or at least, her mother's — made life in Mrs. Simpson's second grade classroom as unpleasant and unavoidable as the rest of the school day.

Finally, the worst had happened: Mandi's classroom sanctuary was no more!

Wanting to derail *another* year-long struggle, this time over religious beliefs, Debra took a rare visit to the school to visit Principal Washington personally. To her face, Mandi's principal assured her that not only would he speak to Millie again, but Millie's parents as well. Debra was far from satisfied, but she knew there was little more she could do.

Unfortunately, Millie's parents responded about as passionately to Principal Washington's brief lecture on "religious freedom" as did their daughter, and the classroom ostracization, intimidation, and humiliation continued unabated.

Finally, toward the end of the year, Millie and her family moved away, and Mandi was once again allowed to have at least one room in East Jefferson Elementary School in which to untense her shoulders and let loose with the occasional smile.

But almost as soon as she rid herself of one problem, another one just as quickly reared its ugly head. No doubt fueled by the fun the Mead brothers were having with little Mandi, a boy named Dante* soon took over where they left off. Three years older than Mandi, and no doubt worlds wiser in the ways of the street, Dante called little Mandi every name in the book, while one particular seemed to be his favorite: Hemorrhoid.

As in, "Here comes Hemorrhoid!"

Or, "Hey, Hemorrhoid Head!"

"Hemorrhoid Face! Hemorrhoid Face!"

It didn't matter what the context, time, date, or place, the word stung Mandi like poison — and stuck to her like glue. For not one week, not two weeks, not one month, but two and a half full months, Dante repeatedly and continuously degraded Mandi with foul language and his one favorite word, mixed in as often as possible — just for good measure!

Two and a half months.

Ten long weeks.

Ten long weeks of abuse, name calling, embarrassment, humiliation, and ridicule. Repeated calls, and visits, to Principal Washington did nothing to stem the tide of abuse. Only one thing could end Dante's reign of terror. Only one thing could shut him up. Only one thing could silence his derision, mockery, and abuse.

Ten long weeks.

Two and a half months.

And, finally, gratefully, fortunately — school was finally out.

And Dante finally quit calling Mandi Wein a hemorrhoid.

But only because he had to...because summer left him without a target.

FOR THE CHILDREN ...
Putting a Stop to Schoolyard Abuse

WHAT TO DO *AFTER* YOUR CHILD HAS BEEN BULLIED:

If your child has been bullied, it is important that she tell someone as soon as possible; her parents, a teacher, a counselor, the principal, or at the very least a friend. When a child becomes a victim of bullying, it is normal to feel upset and afraid, not to mention being embarrassed to talk about it.

Your child has one of two choices: not to talk about it and risk that the situation gets worse, or to talk about it with someone she trusts, either with you, her parents, a teacher, her brother or sister, or even with a friend. Remember to tell her to *talk* about it. By talking, the child will begin to feel better.

Offer her your help. Ask her to talk about it. If she refuses to talk and you detect that something just isn't right, communicate with:

An educator at school if the aggression has taken place there

A coach or supervisor if you think the aggression is taking place during a sport or leisure activity

The bully's parents or any witness if the aggression is taking place in an unsupervised area such as the park or a playground

By regularly exchanging information relating to your child's relationships with others (students, school educators, friends, etc.) your child will feel that she can trust you and will tell you about the things she is dealing with

CHAPTER SIX:
Third Grade

Out with the old, in with the new...

It was the type of news most parents miss, or if they *do* happen to run across it, ignore. After all, who reads any of that "two weeks before school is supposed to start back up again the mailbox fills up with notes from the school" type of stuff anyway? Most of it is just teacher "wish lists" or books your kid should have read over the summer, but most likely didn't.

Average parents just throw it away — or use it to line the bird cage!

But Mark and Debra Wein weren't "average" parents.

Not anymore...

If they received a piece of mail, a newsletter, a memo, a notice, even so much as a cafeteria *menu* from East Jefferson Elementary School, they not only read it, they devoured it!

Such was the case when the announcement that Jefferson was getting a new principal arrived in the mail on one of those last, precious days of summer before Mandi was to start third grade. Mr. Washington was out, and a new principal, Mr. Larcon*, would be taking his place.

Even Mandi smiled at this news, for once again there was a brief flicker of hope at the Wein house. None of them had been too eager to send Mandi back into the "belly of the beast" once school started up in a few short days, but with the new announcement came new hope, and hope was something they all coveted these days.

Debra, particularly, coveted the news that Mandi's school would be run by a new principal. While the notice wasn't full of details, just the fact that Mr. Washington was now out of the picture brought the briefest flicker of a smile to her face. Perhaps they could all rest easy, now.

Perhaps the end of Mandi's torment was finally in sight...

And so it was with unreserved emotion that Debra once again sent her daughter off to the bus stop on the first day of third grade. She watched poor Mandi the whole way, and even until the bus rolled into view. There was no pushing, no shoving, no physical violence of any kind.

"Perhaps," she sighed as she went back into the kitchen to get her other daughters ready for school, "the worst is over and done."

But life at ground zero was very different for little Mandi Wein. She marveled at the inherent evil evidenced by the Mead brothers. For while her mother looked on, they seemed to know it, could actually sense her eyes upon them — even without looking.

Mandi was at first relieved that Skeeter had apparently moved onto the junior high school, though she was surprised he had managed to pass sixth grade when all he had ever cared about was making her life a living hell!

Still, his next to oldest brother Pugsley was taking up right where Skeeter left off. Even as Debra kept a careful lookout from her perch high across the street, Pugsley and another older boy, James Brogan, stood perfectly still a few feet away from her and littered her with vulgar names and vile epithets.

They never advanced on her, never kicked sand down her socks or spat on her or even pushed her. They just stood there, quite calmly, as if they might be reading the morning paper or memorizing poetry instead of cutting her down with their voracious appetite for schoolyard abuse.

Again and again, over and over, the names flew out of the thin slits of their mouths. Mandi was too shocked to appeal to her mother for help, and soon the bus advanced and swallowed them whole. Without the watchful eyes of her mother upon them, Pugsley and James grew more active in their taunts and threats, and it was only after the bus had pulled from the stop and was headed toward school that the abuse began in earnest.

After school that day, after surviving her long eight hours, Mandi told a hopeful and newly disappointed Debra about what had happened, both while she was looking and when she wasn't.

Debra immediately called the new principal, Mr. Larcon, telling him in no uncertain terms that this was the third year in a row that her daughter had suffered abuse right under the former principal's nose, and that she wasn't going to stand for it.

Not this year.

Not ever...

The words sounded vaguely familiar to Debra, if not to Mr. Larcon. For his part, the new principal calmly and quietly told Debra that he would, of course, "take care of the problem."

Debra hoped. She prayed. She hoped some more. Mandi went off to school, came home torn and tattered, and together they prayed some more. Nothing, not one thing, was ever done to either Pugsley or James.

Every day Mandi would return home in tears, revealing an even greater level of violence, threats, and abuse. Every day, Debra would call Mr. Larcon. Every day, Mr. Larcon would assure Debra that he would "take care of the problem."

Every morning the vicious cycle repeated itself.

Finally, Mark took matters into his own hands. *Enough is enough,* he thought as he strode down the street to speak directly to Mr. Mead for himself. He had tried to be calm, tried to remain cool, tried to listen to Debra's prevailing philosophy that the school would handle things if they only followed "the chain of command."

But Mark knew a little something about the chain of command himself, and after waiting patiently for the school, the counselors, the principal, the teachers, anyone to do something about what his daughter was going through, he finally decided to skip a few rungs and go straight to the horse's mouth.

He banged on the door of the Mead house, and was grateful when Mr. Mead himself opened it up. He wasn't sure what he might have done had little Skeeter or Pugsley presented themselves. Not after what they'd put his innocent little daughter through! Mr. Mead was calm. At first. So was Mark. At first. But as the accusations flew and the blame was placed, back and forth, forth and back, Mark knew that he was fighting a losing battle — not only with Mr. Mead, but with his own self-control. For if he had to stand there and listen to a grown man blame a first grader for a fourth, fifth, or sixth grader's actions, he was going to lose his cool.

And that would not be good...

Walking home from a particularly unproductive meeting, Mark resolved that taking matters into his own hands was not in Mandi's best interests. While beating Mr. Mead to a pulp might have made him feel a whole lot better, it wouldn't have changed things for Mandi. Not one bit.

In fact, it might have made matters worse if Mr. Mead had pressed charges and had Mark dragged down to jail! How would Mandi cope with all she was already dealing with, and then her father being arrested for assault on top of it all?

But how could it have ever gotten so bad? How could his daughter be abused, verbally, physically, even sexually, each and every day — and nobody could do a damn thing about it? Wasn't this America? Things like that didn't happen here. Did they?

This was the kind of thing you read about in the paper, or saw on the news, and shook your head at, and felt sorry for some poor bastard a few thousand miles away. "That could never happen here," you always thought. "Not in my town, not in my house, not in my daughter's school."

But here he was, tromping back from the house of the man whose children were calling his daughter names he wouldn't even use in a biker bar! And there wasn't a damn thing he could do about it, short of putting his fist through the man's face and winding up cooling his heels in jail for who knew how long!

And what would that solve? He could just hear the new principal now: "Perhaps school isn't Mandi's real problem. Have you ever stopped to think what living under the same roof with a man convicted of assault and battery might do to a child's self-esteem? Did you ever think that perhaps she was pointing the finger at someone else in order to avoid getting punished herself?"

More legalese. More ten dollar words. More gobbledygook designed to take the emphasis off the school, and put it on the parents. No matter how hard it might have been to control his parental instincts, he would not give the school board the satisfaction. Someone was going to pay for what was happening to his daughter.

If it was the last thing he did . ..

Debra wasn't surprised to hear how Mark's meeting with Mr. Mead went. Yet she was surprised by how Mark had handled himself! If she had been there, she wasn't so sure she would have been able to stay as cool, calm, and collected as her husband obviously had.

She might have come home with blood on her hands!

But as third grade slowly ground on for Mandi and the Weins, it wasn't the Mead brothers or their male accomplices who were the only ones giving Mandi a hard time at East Jefferson Elementary school. Soon a new, sinister face would join the roster of Mandi's abusers, this time a girl.

A girl named Tanya. Tanya. Like Skeeter. Or Pugsley. Or Dante, Tanya was quickly to become a household word for the poor Wein family. But despite the new face, the new name, the new tormentor, Debra could hardly claim that she was surprised.

After all, the kids were only doing what was natural. Left to their devices, the big ones, the strong ones, the mean ones, the bad ones, were always going to pick on the nice ones, the cute ones, the smart ones, the weak ones. It was *Lord of the Flies* all over again.

The only problem was, the kids weren't the ones running the show. The school was full of adults: principal, vice principal, counselors, teachers, assistants, aides, custodians, bus drivers, bus monitors, even a school nurse. Could none of them protect her child? Would none of them lift a finger to show her daughter the smallest sign of decency?

If a dog had been mistreated in much the same manner, the school would have been up in arms. "Animal cruelty!" they would cry. "Pet abuse!" But a first grader, a second grader, and now a third grader wasn't even as worthy of their concern as a pet dog?

No, despite herself, Debra couldn't blame Skeeter. Or his brother Pugsley. Or Dante. Or even Tanya. The teachers looked away. The counselors ignored the problem. Even the principal refused to do anything about the situation. No detentions were ever given out. No suspensions were assigned. No expulsions. Why, there was still no assigned seating on the bus, for heaven's sake!

What signal was this sending? What message was going out to 700 school kids when not one single adult ever bothered to say, "No! What is happening here is wrong. This poor girl is being abused and it is high time one of us put a stop to it!"

Instead, the children were left to draw their own conclusions. To whit: "Well, the teachers don't give a damn. The counselors don't care. The aides and assistants could care less. The school nurse turns a blind eye to Mandi's cuts and bruises. Even the principal just slaps us on the wrist, when he bothers to call us into his office at all. Whoo hoo! On with the show!"

And so a new face entered stage left, a new name was added to the growing roster of children who were allowed, perhaps even encouraged, to torment poor little Mandi. Yet where even the Mead brothers seemed to draw a line in how far they would go in their ongoing torture of young Mandi, this new girl, this Tanya, seemed unsatisfied with the current level of abuse.

Like Emeril Lagasse, she seemed to want to "kick it up a notch."

Oh, she started much like the others did. Though Tanya and her little brother, Jonas, were supposed to go to a bus stop at the bottom of the hill, they must have heard about all the "fun" the Mead brothers were having at Mandi's neighborhood bus stop and figured the extra few blocks up the road was worth the effort for the chance to kick around a third grader until the bus pulled up.

And so, one day, Tanya took over where Skeeter had apparently left off. More dirty names. More mean-spirited threats. Then, as if trying to keep her hands clean while playing dirty, Tanya had her little brother kick Mandi in the leg, then spit on her on the bus, and even pull her hair on several occasions.

Mandi tried to be strong, to stand up to Tanya and her little brother, but apparently the stronger Mandi was, the fiercer Tanya became. Soon her threats became constant, brutal, and overpowering.

Mandi had been afraid to tell her parents, for fear of retribution. But when the little girl could take it no longer, she finally broke down and admitted that Tanya and her brother had been brutalizing and humiliating her on almost a daily basis for going on weeks!

Debra immediately called Mr. Larcon, only to told, yet again, that he would "take care of the problem." But armed with the information that Tanya and her brother were purposefully using the wrong bus stop, she countered with this as a possible solution.

Unfortunately, the principal merely told Debra to call the "bus yard." When Debra did, the folks at the bus yard told her to call "the principal." And so it went. Finally, Mr. Larcon relented and told Debra that he would call the bus yard himself and instruct them to make the change, to say that Tanya and her brother could no longer attend the bus stop in the Wein's neighborhood.

Unimpressed, Debra had no choice but to wait. And wait, and wait some more. After two to three weeks of nearly constant and ongoing abuse at the hands of Tanya, her brother, and their friends, nothing had done about the children riding from the wrong bus stop!

When Debra called Mr. Larcon to inquire about why no changes had been made, the school's new principal told her that he could "never get hold of the girl's parents!" However, Mr. Larcon had a suggestion: Debra could drive Mandi to school as a way to solve the problem.

This was an idea Mark and Debra had toyed with ever since Mandi's abuse began early on in first grade. But both parents had agreed that since the abuse merely began at the bus stop, driving Mandi to and from school would hardly solve the problem. Still, desperate to ease her daughter any amount of suffering, even if it only meant the few minutes she spent at the bus stop each morning, Debra pledged to drive Mandi to and from school.

And that is exactly what she did for the rest of the school year...

Unfortunately, as Debra had always suspected, driving Mandi to school only worsened the problem. Immediately after dropping her off and driving away, Tanya seemed to seek out Mandi as if she had implanted a homing signal somewhere upon her body.

Yet where the threats before had always been just that, threats, now Tanya seemed almost offended by Mandi's absence at the bus stop each morning. Soon the older, stronger, more powerful girl took to smacking Mandi in the back of her head repeatedly, as if steering her up the hallway to school.

Not only was the abuse painful, but clearly evident to the little girl's classmates, who laughed at her and jeered all the while the abuse was being perpetrated. Naturally, the cheers and jeers only seemed to egg the older girl on, making the abuse even more severe and painful.

Until, at long last, a school bell sounded or a teacher rounded the corner or a class started, and Mandi was mercifully left alone. For a while, anyway…

But at recess, Tanya was always there. Quick with a slap or a kick or a huge wad of spit to lodge in Mandi's hair. In the cafeteria, Tanya was always there. Before school. There was Tanya. After school. Tanya was there.

And unlike on TV and in the movies, where a heroic teacher or faithful counselor would step in "just in time" to stop the abuse, the pain and harassment and embarrassment continued on, day after day, recess after recess, lunch after lunch, always without rebuke.

In first grade, in second grade, even during the first few weeks of third grade, Mandi could not quite stop herself from tattling on the children who were making her young school life a living hell. It was what good kids did when bad kids were doing something, well, *bad*!

A kid picked on you. You told your teacher. A kid hurt you. You went to the school nurse. A kid threatened you. You told the school counselor. Things continued to get worse, you finally told the principal.

But the rules were reversed at East Jefferson Elementary School. Telling got you nowhere. In fact, it made things even worse. Mandi noticed straight away that whenever she told her mom something that had happened that day at school, and then her mom talked to Mr. Larcon about it, that the next day things would get worse.

Much worse…

Tanya would somehow know. Despite the fact that she was never punished, never threatened with detention or suspension or God forbid expulsion, Tanya always seemed to know when Mandi had told on her.

And it made the beatings all the more severe, all the more vicious, spiteful, and hateful. "Tell on me, will you?" Tanya seemed to be saying with her repeated smacks upside the head. "Just see what happens when you do!"

Mandi got the message, and quit telling her parents what was going on at school. At first, despite herself, Debra believed that Mr. Larcon, or one of the teachers, or even one of the counselors, was finally doing what they were paid to do. When things grew quiet, when Mandi quit complaining, Debra willed herself into believing that things had finally gotten better.

But soon, too soon, Debra realized that Mandi looked no better, felt no better, seemed no happier, despite the apparent lack of abuse. She still came home ratty and tangled, spit on and rumpled. There was still the odd bruise on her neck, her thigh, her back. Still the occasional rip or tear in her blouse or jeans.

And so Debra would have to drag it out of Mandi each day after school: "What happened to you today, Mandi? Who did this to you? Who tore your blouse? Where did you get that bruise?"

Under the repeated questioning, how could Mandi not confess? Yet despite repeated calls to Mr. Larcon, despite driving her to school each single day, despite picking her up after school the whole year long, the pain and harassment and bedevilment and abuse continued unabated.

Until, unbelievably, it was time for summer to start again.

Debra was so relieved she could hardly stand it. But her happiness was short-lived. Almost as soon as school ended and summer began, Mandi seemed no happier, no less tense, no more relieved than if the alarm was still going off and Debra was shooing her into the family car to go to school.

She seemed jumpy. Tense. Worse than ever. She slept little, dogged by horrible nightmares and restless evenings where sleep came infrequently, if it came at all. Thus her days were spent listlessly watching the television, or reading in her room, where she began taking more and more naps and generally hiding herself away from the rest of the family.

Worse still, Mandi seemed to replace her old childhood friends, who never seemed to come around anymore, with a new friend: food. Cookies and cakes and punch and more cookies became Mandi's constant companion, and Debra felt bad keeping the food away from her.

After all, it was the only thing that made Mandi truly happy!

Yet, deep down, Debra knew that the weight Mandi was gaining over the summer would only make her return to school just that much more miserable. Now, instead of Tanya telling Mandi she dressed in "old lady clothes," as she had done repeatedly during third grade, the vengeful young hooligan could add references to Mandi's weight to her limited library of vocabulary words.

Mandi was nearly house bound that entire summer, and it was a battle royal to get her out of the house, into the car, and out in public. Jerky, jumpy, frazzled, and upset, any trip where Mandi was involved soon became short-lived, making the entire Wein family prisoners in their own home.

Such was the extent of the lasting damage done to her at East Jefferson Elementary School. Debra often wondered how it could go on, and often thought that, if Mr. Larcon could just see how erratic Mandi's behavior had became, if he could just see her irrational behavior in the mall, or in a fast-food restaurant, constantly on guard for someone to hit her, punch her, spit on her, abuse her, he might just get the picture.

Alas, it was Mr. Larcon's summer, too…

But as summer ended and fourth grade dawned near, Mandi's episodes worsened. She slept less and less, and ate more and more.

Dark circles grew beneath her eyes even as her cheeks grew puffy with her worsening girth. Debra knew the signs were a call for help, but what could she do but listen to her daughter, nurture her, *feed* her?

Finally, as the last week of summer dawned hot and moist, Mandi grew more and more vocal about not returning to East Jefferson Elementary School.

"I don't want to go back," she would say.

"Please don't make me go back," she might whine.

And Debra and Mark would do their best to calm their daughter's frazzled nerves, assuage her very real fears, and assure her that "everything would be all right." Even though they had little hope of making their words prove true...

Worse yet, Debra had suffered a crippling fall on the job at her workplace, injuring her back to the point where she could no longer drive little Mandi to school and back. And knowing that she would once again be forced to take the bus made Mandi's nightmares increase by the day, until finally she awoke to the worst nightmare of the summer: Her first day back at school...

FOR THE CHILDREN ...
Putting a Stop to Schoolyard Abuse

HOW TO PREVENT BULLYING:

Though it may be exceedingly difficult for your child — or even you as parents — to prevent bullying, there are certain steps you can take to prevent initial, and future, acts of bullying. Here are a few:

Your child should not carry a large amount of money.

Remind your child not to brag about owning expensive things like a Discman or electronic games.

In the schoolyard, your child should stay where most of the kids are playing. Bullies don't like to have witnesses.

Your child should avoid walking alone. If possible, he should try to walk to and from school with good friends.

If a schoolmate hits your child, he/she should tell a supervisor or a teacher immediately.

When using public transit, he should try to sit near other adults.

CHAPTER SEVEN:
"Help us, please!"

It seemed as if the kids had been waiting for Mandi to come back to the bus stop. As if, while Debra had driven her to and from school during third grade, they would now be able to make for it for all of fourth grade.

The gloves were indeed off, as they say, and Tanya started in almost immediately on that first morning at the bus stop. "Don't even look my way or I'll smack you in your ____-ing face, you fat bitch!"

The words stung Mandi to the core, and soon the rest of the kids at the bus stop joined in. "Don't look at me, either!" her old friends cried. "Me either, fat ass!" cried other children she had never even met before.

It seemed that now the whole school was out to get her, and she had no earthly idea why. Even the "little" kids she had once been able to count on for support joined in, urged on by the morning mob mentality and giving up on the poor girl they had once known and loved.

She was no longer merely Mandi, anymore. She was "that fat bitch," or that "dumb slut who wears old lady clothes," or that "hemorrhoid" or that "loser" or that "tattletale."

In the rigid caste society that is modern day public school, Mandi had joined the ranks of the lowest of the low. She was no longer just a "nerd" or a "goober." No longer just a "brain" or a "geek." She belonged to no group, for none would have her. She sank below the dopers and the druggies and the dead-heads and the cry-babies and the brats and the boogers and the loners and the creeps. She had her own realm, and there she was queen for the day, every day.

She became the school outcast, and there was not one single thing she could do about it.

Was it Mandi's fault? Surely not. What could a first grader have done to deserve the horrific abuse she had suffered those many years ago on her very first day of school? What outfit could she have worn? What statement could she have made? What social blunder could she have blundered to reap this much havoc, abuse, and terror on her tiny little body?

Was it the other children's fault? Partially, perhaps. After all, it's hard not to blame a fourth, fifth, or sixth grader who picks on a first, second, or even third grader. After all, the older kids are supposed to know better. Supposed to protect the little kids. Supposed to stick up for the underdogs. The nerds. The wimps.

At least, that's how it's supposed to work in a "normal" school. A school where a principal takes pride in his young charges and feels morally responsible when one of them, when even a single, solitary one of them, feels afraid to come to his place of business.

That's how it's supposed to work in a school where teachers pay attention to children who complain of being beaten, verbally harassed, threatened, or even sexually assaulted. Where counselors sit up and take notice when they see the same little girl, day after day, week after week, year after school year, sitting in the same seat outside the principal's office to lodge yet another complaint against yet another hoodlum, thug, or ruffian.

That's how it's supposed to work.

In a normal public school...

But it was apparent to the Weins, and more apparent to still to young Mandi Wein, that East Jefferson Elementary School was no "normal" public school. Instead of the principal running the kids, the kids ran the school. They were the ones who said when Mandi could play kickball or not. They were the ones who determined whether Mandi would go home with a bloody nose, or without. They were the ones who made Mandi's day heaven — or hell.

Not the principal. Not the teachers. Not the counselors. Not the school nurse. Not the assistants, not the aides, not the bus drivers, nor any other of the adults who were supposedly "in charge."

The inmates were running the asylum, and Mandi was their hostage!

And at no time was that ever more painfully evident than with the beginning of Mandi's fourth year at East Jefferson. From minute one, from perhaps the very first second that she stepped her foot back on that accursed bus stop, Mandi's life became a living hell.

Again...

It might have been Tanya who started it, but it seemed as many kids as possible were determined to get in the game before the year was out.

And did they ever...

Feeling trapped in another season of The Twilight Zone, Debra called Mr. Larcon and begged with him, pleaded that this year not be a repeat of third grade. Or second grade. Or first grade. Apparently alarmed at what had happened on Mandi's very first day back on the bus, he asked if Debra could simply drive her daughter to school again that year.

When Debra apprised him of her current situation, he amazingly came up with a solution, however short-lived. Mandi could now sit with the bus monitor. Elated, Debra thought that maybe, just maybe, this might be the answer to her long-awaited prayers. The very next morning, Mandi sat with the bus monitor and, while it didn't stop the actual abuse that continued to take place at the bus stop itself, it at least afforded young Mandi the much-needed respite from repeated attacks she had experienced on the bus.

Unfortunately, after only a week of this brief respite, the bus monitor callously told Mandi that she could no longer sit with him, nor could she even sit near him. The front of the bus was reserved for the "little kids," he told Mandi, yet again sending her back into exile in the middle of the bus, where her tormentors sat waiting patiently for her eventual return.

Their suspicions had been right all along: No adult would help

Mandi. Not a single one...

Still trying to keep a brave upper lip, and save herself from added torture, Mandi did not tell her parents that the bus monitor had sent her back to the hands of her abusers. Instead, they believed she was still being protected on the bus, and were unaware of this drastic change.

But they soon had other concerns to worry about. In the recess yard one sunny afternoon, Mandi was surrounded by eight to ten kids who took turns pushing her in the mud, punching her in the stomach, kicking her, and calling her names.

Their ringleader? Not Skeeter, not Pugsley. Not Tanya or even her brother. This time, there was a new face to contend with, new names to be called, new hands to play rough, new feet to kick out. A girl named Karen*, who lived in the same neighborhood as Mandi, started the rout by shoving Mandi down and kicking her, then egging on her ruffian friends.

One can only imagine the stark terror and panic the young girl faced as nearly a dozen older, bigger, stronger schoolchildren vehemently surrounded her and shamed her in the mud, pained her with abuse, and repeatedly demeaned her with their verbal and physical abuse.

One on one, Mandi had always been able to protect herself, at least. Even with two attackers, such as Skeeter and Pugsley or even Tanya and her brother, Mandi had always been able to at least stand her ground. But now she fell victim to the rigors of true mob violence, and there was nothing she could do about it but hope and pray that someone, some adult, might finally, at long last, come to her rescue and stop her abusers from their menacing behavior.

Alas, how could she expect such a logical response at East Jefferson?

Amazingly, a young girl did run over to the nearest teacher and alert this Mr. Phillips*, who was no more than thirty feet away, and told him what was happening. Instead of merely walking the thirty feet to see what all the fuss was about and telling them himself, Mr. Phillips simply told the little girl to tell the kids to "knock it off."

Naturally, when this brave little girl returned to tell the vicious mob what the teacher had said, they merely laughed her off and continued their abuse without pause. For the rest of the recess period.

Which lasted nearly twenty minutes...

For almost half an hour Mandi Wein was repeatedly kicked, punched, shoved, pushed, spat on, and verbally abused with the usual round of hateful epithets and scornful language.

Yet the violence did not end there. Perhaps emboldened by the fact that they had "gotten away with it" at recess, perhaps spurred on by Mandi's resilience, perhaps just wanting to "finish up where they had left off," Karen once again initiated a fight with Mandi at the bus stop when she got home from school that day.

Pushing her as she got off the bus, Mandi watched in vain as the driver merely drove off, ignoring the violence he left in his wake. With no adults to stop her, Karen continued what she had started on the playground earlier that day and viciously clawed Mandi's face and neck before proceeding to give her a black eye with a punch that would have scared even Skeeter or Pugsley half to death!

Fortunately, a neighbor broke up the fight and Debra was alerted to the incident by a concerned neighbor, who told her and gave her the particulars, not only about what had happened at the bus stop after school, but about what had transpired earlier that day at recess.

Incensed, Debra listened as her neighbor explained that Karen's mother had received a phone call earlier that day from school. The concerned mother had been informed that Karen and Mandi had "gotten into it" and to be prepared, because the rumor was that the "fight," if you could call such a one-sided incident that, might spill over to the bus stop after school.

Why Debra had never been informed was a complete mystery, and remains one to this day. After all, who had more to fear: the girl who started the fight, or the girl who'd been threatened within an inch or her life? Who deserved the benefit of the doubt more? The roughneck who had pushed Mandi down on the playground, or the poor, embattled fourth grader who'd been abused from the very first day of first grade?

94

It seemed ludicrous that Debra had not been informed and, worse yet, since this all occurred on a Friday she would have to wait until Monday to sort things out with the school. After tending to Mandi all weekend long, Debra called Mr. Larcon first thing Monday morning and, amazingly, he declared that he "didn't know anything about" the incident on Friday!

Was his memory truly *that* short?

But Debra continued moving forward, undaunted, asking the lackadaisical principal who in his employ had called Karen's mother, during school hours, to warn her of the impending fight? Again, the principal answered that he had no idea. And despite the fact the Mr. Larcon once again told Debra that he would "take care of it," she saw no reason to believe him.

When nothing had been done to Karen four days after the right, Debra took matters into her own hands and called the police, asking what she might do to resolve the situation and protect her daughter from further abuse.

The local police department told Debra to file a complaint, and that a Detective Payton* would go to the school and talk not only to the principal, but the children involved as well.

In the meantime, Mark Wein took over where his wife had left off and began calling Principal Larcon himself. Unfortunately, he was having no luck getting the ever-elusive principal on the phone. After several days of trying, Mark finally caught Mr. Larcon in the office and asked him what he planned to do about Mandi's ongoing situation of abuse and neglect "on his watch."

To which Mr. Larcon rudely replied, "I have seven hundred kids to watch, I can't watch your kid!"

Finally, there was the answer the Weins knew had been lurking just beneath the surface. It had taken four years to bubble over, but the true philosophy of the administration at East Jefferson Middle School had finally spilled over the surface, and straight into the Weins' lap: "I have seven hundred kids to watch, I can't watch your kid!"

Naturally, the words that were unspoken cut straight to the bone: "Those 699 *other* kids are more important than your daughter!"

Mark could hardly believe his ears, and immediately began trying to get in touch with the superintendent of the local school district. He placed several calls, yet none were answered. A week later Mark finally got hold of the superintendent, explained Mandi's ongoing situation of abuse and neglect at East Jefferson, and was told by the superintendent that he would "look into the situation and get back" to Mark.

Another week passed by without result. No phone calls. No Emails. No letters. No memos. Nothing. Finally, the Weins could take it no longer and sought legal counsel. After contacting several attorneys, Mark and Debra chose a lawyer named Charles Sylvester as their man.

After listening incredulously to their four-year long odyssey, Sylvester spoke to Mandi personally and decided to write a letter on behalf of the Weins asking the East Jefferson County School Board to stop the abuse of their daughter. He also requested a meeting with the school's principal, Mandi's teacher, and the Weins. The letter was sent, and never responded to.

Meanwhile, despite the faint glimmer of hope that had invaded her life in the form of Charles Sylvester, Mandi's abuse continued unabated at East Jefferson. In fact, as if they suspected that the end was in sight, Mandi's tiny tormentors seemed to step up the pace before the party did, indeed, finally end.

The first assault happened in Mandi's own classroom, a veritable first. Where before the attacks had happened only at the bus stops, on the bus, at recess, in the halls, or in the cafeteria, now the violence had found its way into her very own classroom.

Finally, at long lost, her one remaining sanctuary had been invaded by the mongrels...

It happened when Ms. Hamburg*, Mandi's fourth grade teacher, left the room to run an errand of some sort. Despite the fact that teachers are never to leave their class unsupervised, Ms. Hamburg apparently thought she'd be gone for fewer minutes than she was actually in absence.

In any event, a classroom ruffian named Chris Keller* quickly attached a "Kick Me" sign to Mandi's back. Immediately, the classroom erupted into uproarious horseplay as their human victim was kicked about the legs, buttock, and even her hand! Almost the entire classroom full of nearly thirty children joined in on the fun, humiliating Mandi to the point of tears, and then far, far beyond.

One minute.

Two minutes.

Five minutes.

Eight minutes.

TEN MINUTES!

For ten to fifteen minutes the abuse continued. Mandi would reach around and rip the sign off when immediately another would materialize out of thin air and attach itself to her back, beginning the abuse all over again.

When Ms. Hamburg finally returned back to the room after her unexcused absence, the class denied anything had happened and the entire incident was apparently written off to "just another Mandi moment!"

Bruised and battered, Mandi did not even have to explain her attack before an outraged Debra was already dialing the direct number to Mr. Larcon's office. Again, the principal said he would "take care of it."

Again, Debra had little hope that he would be true to his word.

And even less recourse…

But just like the incident at the playground, the morning attack only left the hungry mob with a taste for more violence. Several days later, on the bus going home after another brutally, and brutal, long day at school, a female bully by the name of Terri Hawking* grabbed Mandi by her hair, pulled her to the floor of the bus, and dragged her halfway down the aisle, leaving entire patches of hair missing from Mandi's bruised and battered head.

Debra immediately called Mr. Larcon, more upset than ever. "What has to happen?" she asked. "What has to happen before you'll do something for our daughter? Does Mandi have to be *killed* first?"

Unruffled, the stoic principal again told Debra that he would "take care of it." Debra went on to ask if he had received the letter from the Weins' attorney, to which he responded that he was "going to try to set up a meeting."

Naturally, the meeting, nor Terri's punishment, never took place.

Fearing that only the police could help them now, Debra once again contacted the local authorities and filed another police report for this latest outrage. Unfortunately, upon reading the preliminary report, an officer quickly told the Weins that because the incident occurred on school grounds that it was "not a police matter, it's a school matter."

Flippantly, the officer further suggested that Mandi should "take karate."

As things slowly began spiraling out of control for Mandi and the Weins, Mark tried one last-ditch effort at contacting the school superintendent again. After weeks of trying, without any callbacks, Mark finally got hold of the elusive superintendent and asked that, at the very least, Mandi be sent to another school in the same district.

The superintendent briskly suggested that Mark write him a letter and "if I deem it necessary, I'll see what I can do."

Finally, the Weins had had enough. They both knew the letter would go nowhere. They both knew that Mr. Larcon would never lift a finger to help poor Mandi. They knew that no teacher, no counselor, no aide, no nurse had ever been able to stop one simple incident from happening to their daughter, and that she would forever be the pariah at East Jefferson Elementary school.

Given no other choice, they withdrew Mandi from fourth grade and enrolled Mandi in a nearby private school. They hoped the new surroundings, the new school, the new environment, would simply make everything "go back to normal."

But as the Weins were soon to find out, getting back to normal would be impossible for little Mandi. Not without treatment.

Not without intense, professional treatment.

And that was something they simply couldn't afford.

But they knew somebody, or *something*, that could.

The East Jefferson County School Board.

It was about time they paid for what they'd done, or let be done, to their innocent little daughter.

And they would pay dearly…

FOR THE CHILDREN ...
Putting a Stop to Schoolyard Abuse

WHAT TO DO IF YOUR CHILD IS BEING BULLIED:

As a parent, you may feel that the best way to protect your precious child is by confronting the bully, or even the bully's parents, yourself. However, this step may only exacerbate the problem and cause the bullying to intensify. However, there *are* some steps that you can take to help your child cope with school bullies. The following tips can help you protect your child from being bullied.

Look for signs. Many children will not complain about being bullied at school, but will look for ways to avoid attending school and/or after-school activities.

Assess the severity of the situation. If your child has been physically harmed or threatened with physical harm, notify the school immediately, and insist that it take immediate action to protect your child from violence.

Explain the dynamics of bullying to your child. Help him or her understand that bullying comes from the bully's low self-esteem; a bully can only feel big by making others feel small.

Take your child's concerns about bullying seriously. Many children have a tendency to overreact, or even tell "tall tales." But bullying is no laughing matter, and you owe it to your child to take their concerns about being bullied seriously.

Work with your child to brainstorm ways to deal with a less severe bullying situation directly, and help her make a plan. The more you can empower your children to manage their own affairs, the greater their self-esteem will become.

Bolster your child's confidence. Despite their behavior, bullies are basically cowards and gravitate toward easy marks. Encourage your child not to react to a bully's taunts.

CHAPTER EIGHT:
Mandi's Lost Year

Having run out of choices, and at considerable expense to themselves, Mark and Debra Wein pulled little Mandi out of the East Jefferson School System and, in November of 1999, enrolled her in nearby Providence Hebrew Day School, which, according to their impressive Website, offered "Quality Jewish and General Studies in a Warm and Personal Learning Environment."

After four years of enduring endless abuse, repeated beatings, and emotional torment at the hands of fellow students, it might as well have said, "The land of milk and honey!"

Mandi had taken a tour of the school grounds and facilities before her very last day at East Jefferson Elementary School, and both she and her parents agreed that it was the best place for her. With its structured setting and nurturing staff, Debra immediately felt a flood of relief wash over her as she filled out Mandi's paperwork in preparation for her first day of private school.

Naturally, Debra worried about her middle daughter and her new school environment. After having such a bad experience at East Jefferson, how could she not? But even in the first few days, Debra could see a marked difference in her daughter's behavior.

While the battle scars were still there — Mandi was still not sleeping through the night and leaving the house, at any time, let alone the morning before another day at school, still provided numerous challenges — Debra could tell that, perhaps for the very first time, Mandi felt...*safe*.

The battle-weary, distrustful little girl who had endured so much, and been betrayed yet again, by child and adult alike, even started making...*friends*. Debra was no less than thrilled to hear Mandi talking almost daily about other children, without following their names with statements like, "So and so...pulled my hair," or "So and so...beat me up" or "So and so...dragged me across the classroom."

Slowly, the circles under Mandi's eyes began to soften and the playful side of her personality began making appearances, however brief, at the breakfast and dinner tables every so often.

Still, Debra could not forget the injustices done to her daughter in the local public school system to which she had entrusted her for four long years. Seeing the difference in Mandi, the pleasant school surroundings she was now inundated with, the caring staff and well-behaved children, only served to highlight the unpleasant and disastrous effects of East Jefferson Elementary School all the more severely.

Like awakening from hibernation, Debra was able to see just how bad things had gotten, now that they were finally "good" again. Watching Mandi giggle with a new friend on the phone or gush about plans for yet another birthday party or sleepover for the coming weekend literally gave Debra the chills.

On one hand, she was thrilled to see her daughter so happy.

On another, she couldn't help but feel guilty that she had had to wait so long for that happiness to arrive...

Soon enough, however, the cracks in Mandi's armor began showing, and the telltale signs that the Weins weren't yet out of the woods began to rear their ugly heads, often at the most inopportune moments.

While her behavior at school remained impeccable and her classroom grades just as good, and while her friendships continued to hold strong even as 1999 faded slowly into 2000, as the New Year began so did Mandi's outward signs of several long and enduring conditions she would suffer as a result of her ongoing torment and abuse at East Jefferson Elementary School.

As January progressed and the successful school year at

Providence Hebrew Day School continued, Mandi slowly began manifesting old habits in new and occasionally disturbing ways. Her sleep again began being disturbed by violent nightmares of other children abusing her.

Night after night, the ghosts of elementary school past haunted her every sleepless moment. In nightmares that left her shaking and drenched in sweat, Mandi ran from her tormentors. The faces from her past were as clear as day to the battle-scarred little girl — and just as dangerous in the dark as they were in the day.

Perhaps even more so...

With the decrease in sleep came an increase in irritability, which was often directed at her younger sister, Victoria. She began eating more to assuage her feelings of instability and nervousness, and Debra watched silently as Mandi gained pound after pound.

Debra also noticed a new trend in Mandi's behavior, a sudden urge to have absolute order, with everything in its place and a place for everything. Her dresser drawers, her desktop, even her stuffed animals, were ceaselessly arranged and then rearranged. Once she even lashed out at her little sister because she had put one of the crayons back in the box...upside down!

Becoming increasingly compulsive, she bathed often, too *often*, irrationally complaining of body odor that no one else could smell. Her clothes needed to be just as clean, forcing Debra to do untold loads of laundry a day in vain effort to keep Mandi on an even keel.

Debra consulted the faculty and staff at Providence Hebrew Day School and, while she was relieved to hear that Mandi's grades were still above average, her behavior was to be commended, and her peer relationships were still "good," she felt at a loss to explain Mandi's troublesome behavior at home.

Eventually, the Weins felt powerless in the face of Mandi's increasingly "anti-social" behavior and disturbing emotional outbursts. After careful advisement and much research into their options, Mark and Debra sought professional help for their emotionally unstable daughter.

They finally chose Ronald Oakley, LICSW, of the Providence

Center, a local psychiatric organization offering "metal health and substance abuse care and treatment services for adults, children, adolescents, and families."

By this time Mandi had begun to come apart at the seams, her carefully constructed world falling apart by degrees as her tenuous hold on reality slowly eluded her tiny little grasp. For so long she had tried to battle the demons within, somehow managing to fight them back through sheer will or force of her formerly strong and resourceful personality.

Finally, she could no longer fight her inner battles alone...

The Progress Notes from Mandi and the Weins first few meetings with their therapist, Ronald Oakley, reveal just how bad the situation had gotten:

"[Mandi is]... showing symptoms of OCD (Obsessive Compulsive Disorder) and perhaps PTSD (Post-traumatic Stress Syndrome)."

****

"Parents report an increase in paranoia... Mandi said she feels strangers are 'dangerous' and is hypervilgilent."

****

"Mother continues to report OCD symptoms such as Hyper-religiosity and scrupulosity, as well as compulsive behavior such as taking off her glasses every time the school bus passes a certain group of children on the street (who do not know her. She says they only look at her...no one else on the bus)."

****

"Mother started the session by saying she has been noticing Mandi has been increasingly paranoid, i.e.: believing cars might be following them, etc."

****

"Mandi's symptoms worsened after our last session. After the session, she tantrummed about not being able to eat two hamburgers instead of one."

****

"At home, she eats a great deal and 'steals' from the refrigerator..."

****

"Throughout the session, [Mandi] is 'silly' and makes immature gestures and tries to engage her mother through acting out."

Home wasn't the only place Mandi was "acting out," however. At Providence Hebrew Day School, Mandi's emotional baggage eventually caught up with her and her carefully constructed façade began cracking around the edges. No longer were her grades flawless, her behavior impeccable, her friendships secure.

As the world between fantasy and reality, nightmare and daytime, began overlapping, the borders of her loosely controlled world closed in on her, leaving her no choice but to "lash out" and "act up."

Lately, Mandi's emotions had introduced themselves in the form of overeating, and soon she began to gain weight. Food became a source of both comfort and concern, both an obsession and a compulsion, and shortly Debra began receiving complaints from the private school about Mandi's having stolen items, such as ice cream or candy bars, from both the school cafeteria and even other students in her classroom.

Not mature enough to recognize her obvious cries for help, her peers were confused and, naturally, upset by Mandi's actions. Her friendships began to deteriorate and, as the Obsessive Compulsive

Disorder and even Post-traumatic Stress Syndrome took hold of young Mandi's life, her behavior soon spiraled out of control.

Long, extended crying jags were not uncommon, both in and out of the home. When Mark and Debra punished her by sending her to bed early, she could be heard literally "sobbing" for up to two hours at a time. Defiance alternating with being over-apologetic soon became the norm of the day as Mandi's moods swung from high to low and back to high again. No one escaped Mandi's wrath, and few outside of the professional field of psychiatry could cope with her outrageous behavior.

The Weins soon felt like they had lost control of their own daughter. Like a bull in a china shop, Mandi controlled the emotional well-being of the Wein house. The family walked around on eggshells, constantly worried that their actions, their statements, even an innocent remark, might "set Mandi off" and throw the house into emotional turmoil.

But it wasn't just the Weins who had lost control. In the end, Mandi's behavior became too troublesome for the private school in which she had enrolled, so full of high hopes, only one year earlier. In November of 2000, she was officially released from Providence Hebrew Day School and asked not to return for the winter semester.

But being kicked out of her once safe haven was only the beginning of Mandi's mounting troubles. The medication prescribed for Mandi's various diagnoses was soon spiraling out of control as well. Paxil. Celexa. Topamax. Clomipramine. Hydrxyne. At over $100 a month per prescription, the bills for Mandi's care soon became nearly as outrageous as her escalating behavior!

In his Treatment Summary, which would later be introduced into evidence in Mandi's trial, Clinical Director for the Providence Center Dr. Frank S. Shaffer* wrote, "Mandi is a 10-year-old female who was initially evaluated in March of 2000. At that time she presented to The Providence Center with complaints that she had been experiencing periods of fearfulness, sadness, and anxiety along with hyper-vigilance and some compulsive behaviors.

"Her family had reported that she had been physically and verbally abused by children in her previous school placement over a several year period. As noted in my initial evaluation, the abuse reportedly consisted of constant teasing and harassing, as well as repeated beatings and at least one occasion in which she was reported as having been 'stabbed in the private area with a pencil.'

"Mandi had moved to a different school, Providence Hebrew Day School, and initially had seemed to adjust well in that setting. A variety of other behavioral concerns had been identified, which included continued hyper-vigilance in her old neighborhood, fearfulness, a new pattern of aggressive behaviors directed towards her younger sister, persistence of depressed mood, and the emergence of some compulsive behaviors.

"She had had an increase in appetite with a 20-pound weight gain and had a decrease in her energy level, worsening of her sleep pattern, and intrusiveness memories of the trauma she experienced in school as well as nightmares about children mistreating her. Increased irritability and decreased interest in previously pleasurable activities was also noted.

"Mandi was assigned a diagnosis of Post Traumatic Stress Disorder with depressed mood, and concerns around possible Obsessive Compulsive Disorder were also noted. She was placed on Paxil in an attempt to address these symptoms. Paxil was changed the following month to Celexa after she developed increasing irritability and emotional liability as well as suicidal ideation. On Celexa she continued to demonstrate unstable mood and present reported 'extreme highs and lows' with periods of giddiness and also periods of sadness as well as increasing conduct problems and aggressive behaviors. Celexa was increased to 30 mg per day but was discontinued in July of 200 because of a lack of response.

"A pattern of more clearly-defined obsessive compulsive concerns emerged over this time, and a trial of Anafranil was initiated. Anafranil continues to be prescribed currently at a level of 100 mg per day. On this level she has obtained low therapeutic levels of Clomipramine and Norclominpramine (220).

"A trial of Depakote was initiated in September because of

continuing mood fluctuations possibly indicative of Bipolar Disorder. The Depakote was discontinued the following month because of a lack of response at therapeutic blood levels, and a trial of Zyprexa was initiated. Currently she receives Zyprexa, 5 mg at bedtime..."

It was clear that Mandi's care had become too much for the Weins to bear, and again and again the cause of her symptoms was as clear as the totals on the prescription bills that piled up, unpaid, on the Weins' kitchen counter each month: East Jefferson Elementary School.

After months of procrastinating, worrying about making the sordid details of Mandi's ordeal public knowledge, and fretting over the nearly insurmountable cost, Mark and Debra Wein agreed: It was time to seek legal representation and sue the East Jefferson County School Board.

FOR THE CHILDREN ...
Putting a Stop to Schoolyard Abuse

HOW CAN I TELL IF MY CHILD IS BEING BULLIED AT SCHOOL?

Oftentimes, children feel embarrassed or even profoundly ashamed to admit that a bully is picking on them at school. Therefore, they might not confess about what might be happening to them. Not right away, anyway. However, you can investigate for yourself and, through careful observation, see a few tell-tale signs that might mean your child is being victimized by a bully. Things to look out for include:

Changes to usual travel routines
Reluctance to travel to school alone
Excuses to avoid school: tummy aches, headaches, etc.
Standards of school work declining
Crying before sleep
Stammering
Nightmares
Starting to steal
Unexplained cuts, bruises, and scratches

CHAPTER NINE:
Judgment Day

The United States District Court for the District of Rhode Island resides in the US Federal Building and Courthouse, located between Fulton and Washington Streets on the north end of Kennedy Plaza in downtown Providence. Its imposing five-story frame is clad entirely in pristine gray granite.

Its mission statement is equally impressive: "The mission of the U.S. District Court for the District of Rhode Island is to provide an impartial and accessible forum for the just, timely and economical resolution of legal disputes within the jurisdiction of the Court, to protect individual rights and liberties, to preserve judicial independence, and to promote public trust and confidence in the judicial system."

Occupying an entire city block, it originally housed The Providence Post Office, Court House and Custom House. While the post office and customs have since found other lodging, the building now houses a maze of rooms both large and small, devoted almost entirely to courtrooms and those used for court administration offices.

Steeped in history, it is the epitome of the classical Beaux Arts style design favored for monumental public buildings at the turn of the century. Construction began in 1904 by the local architectural firm of Clarke & Howe, and was completed on October 1, 1908 for a cost of $355,200. Boasting limestone from Indiana, marble from Vermont, and woodwork from Ohio, the granite behemoth also features a breathtaking mezzanine level between the first and second stories. A large central court light provides natural illumination to center portions of the top four floors.

It was inside this storied setting that the Weins found themselves in the summer of 2001. Flanked by her lawyer and her husband, Debra Wein was smack dab in the middle of what would eventually become known as: *MARK PASSARELLI AND DEBRA WEIN Individually and as parents and next friends of MANDI PASSARELLI, PLAINTIFFS, VS. TOWN OF JEFFERSON, by and through its Finance Directory, NANCY PERRY, MARCUS WASHINGTON individually and in his capacity as an employee of the Jefferson School Department, DENNIS LARCON, individually and in his capacity as an employee of the Jefferson School Department and PHILLIP MACKEY, individually and in his capacity of Superintendent of the Jefferson School Department, JOHN DOE, individually and in his capacity as an employee of the Jefferson School Department, DEFENDANTS.*

It was a long title for what would prove to be an even longer trial...

While butterflies filled her stomach, Debra felt confident in her choice of a trial lawyer. A local boy, Charles D. Sylvester, Esquire, had been born on November 10, 1950, in Pawtucket, Rhode Island. A trial lawyer specializing in family law, Sylvester had received his Bachelor of Arts Degree at Brown University in 1972, followed shortly thereafter by his Juris Doctor at Georgetown University Law Center in 1975.

Having been published in the *Suffolk University Law Review* and by both the National Business Institute and Lorman Education Services, Sylvester had been a member in good standing of both the American and Rhode Island Bar Associations since 1975.

As the inevitable foreplay of a modern American legal proceeding devoured most of the morning, Debra all but ignored the macho posturing and legalese that filled the air of the storied courtroom like so much cheap perfume. Instead, she looked at the marble walls and rich, oak adornments of the judge's bench and marveled at how she had arrived at such a preposterous and precarious position.

Having taken four years to admit defeat at East Jefferson

Elementary School, Debra Wein was still not one to anger quickly, nor act in haste. Never in a million years had she pictured herself sitting on the opposite side of the defense table from the East Jefferson School Board.

Why, it just wasn't done!

In her day, Debra had gone to school and come home facing an evening of homework. No "ifs," "ands," or "buts" about it. Teachers were strict, principals even more so, and parents bought the company line and backed up both 100%.

Students said "yes, ma'am," and "no, sir," and, if they didn't, they stood in the corner until they'd learned their lesson, or learned it in the principal's office — on the swinging end of a wooden paddle!

But that had been back in her day...

Before crack babies and welfare mommies and the Internet. Before newspapers could print teachers' salaries so that families, including the children, could laugh over them at the breakfast table before school. Before frivolous lawsuits and petty injunctions stripped schools of any real power, and left them full of little more than underpaid baby-sitters who had long since lost the respect of their students.

Into this new world of public education had gone Mandi Wein. "Into the jungle," as it were. Gone was the respect, gone was the fear, gone was the recourse the adults had in the building to do anything about the children.

And such were the consequences. Now all Debra could do was hope, and wait, and pray for judgment.

But first would come the trial...

FOR THE CHILDREN ...
Putting a Stop to Schoolyard Abuse

HOW *YOU* CAN HELP YOUR CHILD

One of the best ways to support your child is to arm them with strategies to deal with bullying behavior. At least then they have something concrete to work with. Try the following:

Tell them that the best way to thwart a bully is to ignore the taunts and walk away. Role play doing this with your child as the bully, you as the victim, and then change roles.

Think about why your child is being bullied. Is it because she needs to develop new social skills? Help her make new friends and build up her confidence.

Discuss with your child when the bullying tends to take place and how to avoid being in the wrong place at the wrong time.

Reassure her that telling, and keeping on telling someone at school about the bullying, will help school staff to offer protection and support where it is needed. It's important that you, and your child, believe that bullying should not be tolerated. No one should have to put up with being in fear at school, and there are things that can be done to make your child feel safe.

CHAPTER TEN:
Order in the Court?

But if Mark and Debra Wein were looking for the old-fashioned, Perry Mason ending to their long ordeal, they were to be robbed even of that. As this was a preliminary hearing to decide culpability on behalf of the Jefferson School Department, the Weins' appearance in court that day was merely formality.

Like bookends, the Weins would be required to appear in court only twice: before and after. Meanwhile, lawyers for both sides would depose Mandi's school secretary, her school nurse, each one of her teachers, grades 1-4 at East Jefferson Elementary School, her two principals, Drs. Washington and Larcon, the superintendent for Jefferson Public Schools, and, finally, themselves.

Most of the depositions took pace at "the scene of the crime," East Jefferson Elementary School itself. Throughout the summer of 2001, lawyers for both sides, a court reporter, and any legal representatives the subject being deposed required would convene at the school or school department for the following depositions.

And, though he was denied the legal wranglings and theatrical drama provided by a courtroom ending, the Weins' lawyer, Charles Sylvester, proved himself to be a worthy adversary for the Jefferson County School Board.

With calm, calculated questioning, his case was quickly built by moving chronologically through each deposition, and then comparing the deposed's story with the Weins. Rarely did it match. But through cunning and precision, Sylvester was able to show that there was indeed abuse suffered at East Jefferson Elementary School, and that whether or not they were responsible for any of it or not, those charged with keeping Mandi Wein, and hundreds of other public school students, safe were at the very least negligent in performing their sworn duties.

What follows are excerpts from actual court documents, as well as commentary on how each witness helped, or hurt, the Weins' case:

THE SCHOOL SECRETARY'S TESTIMONY

Madeline Cartwright* was deposed on June 5, 2001 at 11:05 a.m. She has worked for the Jefferson School Department for twenty-one years as an elementary school secretary, 16 of them at East Jefferson Elementary School.

It will soon become clear why Ms. Cartwright was not only deposed, but crucial to Sylvester's* case. As the school secretary, Cartwright was the conduit through which all of Debra's messages, both verbal, personal, and written, traveled.

In the politics of elementary school, the principal may be the head of the party, but the school secretary is the heck. And she can turn the head any way she so chooses. While Sylvester's gentle questioning yielded little of shock value, it certainly proved that Cartwright, like every single witness to follow, was towing the company line to keep her job with the Jefferson County School Board safe and secure:

[*Any and all questions, or **Q**'s, come from the Weins' attorney, Charles D. Sylvester.]

Q: Starting in the school year of September of 1996 to 1997 … I'm wondering if you had any telephone conversations with the mother during that period of time?

A: I don't recall any messages, any phone calls from Mrs. Wein. The only time I remember phone calls is when Mandi was in the fourth grade.

Q: So for the first, second and third grades you don't have a recollection of any phone calls from Mrs. Wein; is that correct?

A: No. Right. Right.

Q: Did you ever meet with — did you ever see Mrs. Debra Wein during the first, second or third grades?

A: I've seen her, but — I don't recall, you know, the exact time frame.

Q: And...do you know what the subject matter was of those phone calls?

A: Well, she would call and say that Mandi was being picked on by the other children. And I would say, like I normally say when someone calls, I would say, "Did she report it to the recess teacher?" And she would say, "No." And I said, "Well" — and then if it happened in the cafeteria, I would say, "Did you report it to the cafeteria teacher?" And she would say, "No." And, you know, she would call after.

And then I would ask Mr. Larcon. I would say, "Well, did Mandi, you know, talk to you?" And he would say, "I went over to Mandi and I would say, 'How are you doing today?' And she said, 'Fine,' big smile, and that would be it." Or you know, he would say to her at recess, "Did you have a good recess" and she would say, "Yes." And then we would get the phone call from Mrs. Wein saying that Mandi was being picked on or she was hit. And then I would say, "Did she go to the nurse?"

Q: And the subject matter was complaints that Mandi was being picked on, true?

A: Right.

Q: What types of things did she tell you had happened to Mandi?

A: She would say that they were ganging up on her or hitting her. And that's when I would say if she was hurt, did she go to the nurse? And sometimes she would say no.

Q: Did [the mother] ever tell you anything in person?

A: I don't think so. I don't remember her coming in and complaining.

Q: You don't recall conversations, seeing her personally?

A: I saw her personally, but I can't remember for what reasons.

118

Q: How was she with you?

A: She was always polite to me, you know.

The implications of Cartwright's testimony are subtle, but resounding: By her own admission, she doesn't have a recollection of any phone calls from Mrs. Wein, at all! Later testimony from Debra herself, as well as other school employees, reveals that Debra called the school to talk to the principal, either Dr. Washington or Dr. Larcon, at least "three times a week," actually speaking to the principal at least "two times a week," throughout all 4 grades that Mandi attended at East Jefferson Elementary School.

Clearly, someone is lying...

Meanwhile, Sylvester quietly lets the secretary tie her own noose, of a sort, with the admission "And I would say, like I normally say when someone calls, I would say, 'Did she report it to the recess teacher?'" The implication, and it starts with the school secretary and threads throughout the depositions to follow, is thus: The buck definitely does not stop HERE!

Shrewdly, though preserved for every in these very court documents, Cartwright distances herself from any and all responsibility by not only passing the buck to her principal, but the recess teachers, the classroom teachers, the bus drivers, anyone and everyone but herself.

It will soon become a recurrent theme throughout the testimony to follow: It wasn't my responsibility. Yes, I heard complaints. Yes, I knew something was going on. Yes, I heard the rumors. No, it wasn't my job, my duty, my responsibility to intervene.

Meanwhile, a little girl waited, in vain, for an adult, any adult, to stop the madness she endured on a daily basis.

Unfortunately, the adults were all too busy covering their butts...

THE SCHOOL NURSE'S TESTIMONY

Sally Murphy* was deposed on May 31, 2001 at 10:15 a.m. She

has worked for the Jefferson School Department for eleven years as a certified elementary school nurse/teacher, five of them at East Jefferson Elementary School. She has a master's in education and an R. N. degree.

Murphy's testimony, like the school secretary's, is vital to Sylvester's case. As co-workers in the office of East Jefferson Elementary School, these two women were on the front line of defense for children like Mandi Wein. Murphy, especially, would have been privy to any scrapes, cuts, bruising, or other injuries little Mandi might have sustained during her four years of abuse at East Jefferson Elementary School.

But, like Cartwright, Murphy swiftly and surely falls into line with the same old story: "It wasn't me!"

Q: Now, you spoke to Marcus Washington [Mandi's former principal] fairly recently about the subject matter of this litigation; is that true?

A: I don't recall. Several months ago maybe.

Q: And what did he say in the course of that telephone call?

A: He wanted to know if I recalled an incident with Mandi in the school yard with a pencil, and I didn't recall the pencil. I recall an incident, but it was not with a pencil…and he asked me if I recalled an incident with Mandi and another boy that we had — he and I had talked to the children. You know, I was in the room with him when he talked to the children.

I said that I — initially I didn't recall. And then I gave it some more thought and I called him back and said, yes, in fact I did recall sitting with him and he and I speaking to two children. I could not tell you who the children were because it was some time ago, but I know it did not involve a pencil. MY recollection was it was a stick involved.

Q: And what happened during the course of that meeting?

A: Basically we talked to the children. He did most of the talking. It was a boy and a girl. The boy had picked up a stick and was running with it and — being a little boy, and apparently poked Mandi in her bum, the back from what I recall. And we talked to the kids about being safe and not poking people and you could hurt people...

Q: And you did not witness the incident?

A: Correct.

Q: Do you know who, if anybody, did witness the incident?

A: No.

Again, the gist is clear: "I knew something, but not enough. It was an accident. It wasn't my fault, the kids were just playing, and no, nobody ever saw it." Meanwhile, it is equally apparent that Sylvester doesn't have much to work with as to this witness. The majority of her testimony has to do with the "stick incident" in which Mandi was terrorized by a male playmate and stabbed in her "private area" with a stick.

At the same time, Sylvester works hard to prove that, despite the fact that Mandi was not a "complainer," her injuries — both physical and emotional — were very, very real. It would have been so much better for Sylvester's case had Mandi gone to the nurse every time she was assaulted. Had Debra Wein contacted the nurse every time Mandi visited her. Had Mandi's wounds been more visible, more apparent, more shocking.

But as we have already seen, Mandi learned early on that "telling only makes it worse." A quick trip to the nurse, a few names on a pad of paper, a bandage, and Mandi is sent right back to the lion's den. And then what?

What does her complaining, her tattling, get her then? But more abuse on the way home. On the bus. At the bus stop. And where is the school nurse then? Where is the school secretary? Where is anyone and everyone who is supposed to protect her then?

TESTIMONY FROM MANDI'S FIRST GRADE TEACHER

Mona Frank* was deposed on May 31, 2001 at 11:06 a.m. She has worked for the Jefferson School Department for ten years as a first grade teacher, eight of them at East Jefferson Elementary School. She has a master's degree in education as well as an R. N. degree.

Since Mandi did not attend kindergarten at East Jefferson Elementary School, Mona Frank is her first foray into the world of public school. Her very first teacher, if you will. But as the following sworn testimony will show, she teaches Mandi the most important rule of life at East Jefferson Elementary: *It's not **my** responsibility...*

Q: What type of student was [Mandi]?

A: Academically she was probably an average to low-average-ability learner. She was typically an off-task learner. She was very easily distracted. She didn't attend kindergarten, so she was missing a lot of the literacy skills that she would have attained in kindergarten. She received reading recovery help second semester in school, which is for children who are at the lower end of the population in the area of reading.

Q: How was she in terms of behavior?

A: Mandi was very impulsive. She talked out of turn a lot. She was respectful to me but wasn't always respectful of her peers' needs. She argued often with the other children and didn't interact socially the way we would hope a first grader would act.

She had a hard time taking turns. She often would take the things of other children and then not admit to taking them. And then we would have to sit down and say, "Mandi, if you want to make friends, the right thing to do is to ask before you take things. And then when they ask for them back, you need to give them back." So we did a lot of modeling, a lot of behavioral management regarding getting along with others.

Another recurring theme in the testimony from Mandi's teachers was that she was a "behavior problem." Sylvester is quite adept at being objective and letting Mandi's former teachers be as honest as they would like, if not a little more so than usual. There is the further feeling that, because they're not actually sitting across from Mandi in her parents in a traditional courtroom while they give their testimony, that they feel even more free to discuss her behavior at length.

Again, the implication is clear: Mandi was no innocent...

Q: And you don't have any knowledge about anything that happened at the bus stop or on the bus; is that true?

A: *That's right. I don't take care with the bus issues. That would be directed directly to our administrator.*

Q: Are you aware of any pushing or hitting Mandi by any other students during the first grade?

A: There was one incident that occurred during recess time. It happened on a day that I was not in school. They were playing at recess and a little boy had a branch of a tree and he was chasing the girls. And I'm not quite sure how it played out, but somehow she got poked with a stick.

Q: Who witnessed the boy with the tree branch?

A: I don't know. I wasn't there.

Q: So Dr. Washington told you it had happened. But did you ever talk to anybody who actually witnessed what had actually transpired at recess on that occasion?

A: *No, because I wasn't responsible for taking care of that incident. Dr. Washington took care of that incident.*

Q: Where was she hit?

A: From what I recall, she was hit in her private area.

Q: And I have to be specific about what you're referring to. Do you know, when you say a private area —

A: I'm assuming it was below her belly button.

Q: And so the incident was significant enough that the next day there was a meeting with you and the nurse about it; is that correct?

A: There was a meeting with the nurse, Dr. Washington, and I because the little boy's parents were so upset with how it was handled.

Q: What were they upset about?

A: They were upset that Dr. Washington had gone to the extreme of calling the mom at work, or calling the mom at home. And she felt that it was taken out of context because he wasn't a malicious little boy. He wasn't doing things intentionally to harass her. She felt that the stick just landed where it landed, and he did not intentionally hit her in that area with the stick.

So I was told about it because of how upset his parents were so that I would be able to respond to them if they commented. I heard nothing from Mrs. Passarelli regarding the incident.

Q: And...you never witnessed any cursing or swearing or profanities or sexual epithets being applied to her by other students?

A: Not applied to her. She used the profanity.

Q: She did?

A: She did.

Q: What did she say?

A: I can't recall, but Mandi was a very street-wise little girl, more so than many of the other children in my class. And she often said things that were inappropriate.

Q: Did you discuss that with her parents?

A: I'm sure that I did. It was discussed at length with Mandi. Oftentimes I don't call a parent if someone curses. I'll deal with it myself.

Twice Mandi's first grade teacher absolves herself of culpability. "I don't take care with the bus issues. That would be directed directly to our administrator," and "No, because I wasn't responsible for taking care of that incident. Dr. Washington took care of that incident."

While all schools have protocol and procedures, and both the staff and administration at East Jefferson Elementary School continually harp on the fact that there are "700 kids to take care of," 700 is not exactly a mind bogglingly big number. Not like 1,700 or 7,000. In fact, in a K-6 grade school, such as East Jefferson Elementary, that's little more than 100 students per grade!

Hardly a number that would allow a little girl like Mandi Wein to slip through the cracks easily. Ask any teacher and they'll tell you, whether they're at a school with 700 or 1,700 students — the squeaky wheel gets the grease. And complaints from a girl like Mandi Wein are definitely louder than squeaks.

Yet, as evidenced in the above testimony, her teachers use protocol and procedure to self-exonerate themselves from any wrongdoing. Little more than 100 students in first grade and Mandi's own teacher couldn't take it upon herself to talk to the bus driver? To the other teachers at recess? To her own principal? On the poor girl's behalf?

It's not the numbers that are mind-boggling here, it's the callousness...

TESTIMONY FROM MANDI'S SECOND GRADE TEACHER(S)

Megan Potter* was deposed on June 5, 2001 at 12:57 p.m. She has worked for the Jefferson School Department for twelve years as a second grade teacher, all of them at East Jefferson Elementary School.

Second grade was another strange year for Mandi. Not only because she was, yet again, continually assaulted, both verbally and physically, throughout her second year at East Jefferson Elementary School, but because not one but *two* second grade teachers let her slip through the cracks.

Sharing a second grade classroom, co-teachers Nancy Potter, whose testimony follows immediately, and Kathy Kirkland, whose testimony comes after Potter's, both had Mandi during her second year at East Jefferson. Unfortunately, this division of responsibilities only helped to dilute the opportunities for poor Mandi's rescue:

Q: Where did you see [Mandi's] mom, at the school I would assume?

A: Yes. She would pick up her daughter, and I would see her as she picked up her daughter after school hours.

Q: Did you ever have any conversations with her when she picked Mandi up?

A: Many conversations.

Q: During the course of those conversations did she ever complain to you that Mandi had been bothered by any of the other students?

A: Not any one particular child. It would be — we often talked about her getting along with other children. *That was a problem that Mandi had.*

Q: What things did she say to you when you had those conversations with her?

A: The one that stands out most in my mind was in December of that school year, because her daughter — she came to school and talked about her daughter being Jewish. And that was my first time I realized she was Jewish. I didn't know that. And I told her mother I did not realize she was Jewish.

My first feeling, just my opinion, was that she was accusing me of not liking Jewish people. That was the feeling I had. I don't know why I had that feeling, but it was jut a feeling. Okay. But I do know she said other children — this is a fact. I do know she said other children were bothering her about being Jewish.

Q: So you had a conversation with Mandi's mom where she complained to you that other children were giving Mandi a hard time about the fact that she is Jewish; is that true?

A: That's true, yes.

Q: What did Mandi's mom say to you about what the other children were saying to Mandi?

A: The feeling I had was that Christmas was coming. The other children did not understand why Mandi wasn't celebrating Christmas. But she said Mandi came home upset about the children saying that she was Jewish.

Once again, one of Mandi's teachers not only is eager to point out that Mandi had "problems" socializing with other students, but also that she felt threatened by Debra because of her ethnicity, or feelings she had as a result of Debra's ethnicity. The "Jewish incident" related here only further serves to illuminate the bottom line at East Jefferson elementary: The real problem wasn't the other kids, or the teachers, or even the administration, it was…the Weins.

****

126

Kathy Kirkland* was deposed on May 31, 2001 at 1:00 p.m. She has worked for the Jefferson School Department for fourteen years as a second grade teacher, five of them at East Jefferson Elementary School. Sharing a room with Nancy Potter, Kirkland's testimony proves only that even with two pairs of eyes supposedly watching over Mandi Wein, neither of them could see fit to help her:

Q: And how was the responsibility split up between you and Nancy Potter in terms of teaching the class?

A: We split the week. So I would work the first two days, Monday, Tuesday. And Nancy would work Thursday, Friday. And we would alternate the Wednesdays.

Q: Do you recall Mandi's mom, Debra Wein?

A: Mm-hmm.

Q: And do you recall any conversations that you had with Mandi's mom during that school year, the second grade?

A: Somewhat. I remember…one time I stopped her because Mandi had taken cough drops from my desk, a large number over a period of a few days. And she had eaten them and left all the wrappers in her desk. And she denied it, but the evidence was there. And so I spoke to the mom.

And other times maybe — we didn't have a lot of conversations, but we also talked about how she was having trouble getting along with the other children. Stealing was an issue. She was taking things. And for the children in the second-grade level, they don't like children that take their things and then deny it. So we talked about that.

Q: Did Mandi's mom ever complain to you that Mandi had been assaulted or hit or pushed or sworn at by other children, that she had been injured by other children?

A: Not to my recollection, no.

Q: So you never had any conversations with her about anything that may have transpired at the bus stop or on the school bus; right?

A: If she had said something about the school bus, which she may have on one occasion, I would have just said, "We don't really deal with what happens on the school bus." I would have referred

127

her to the principal. So I wouldn't have had that conversation with her. She might have mentioned it once, but that would have been it.

And so, in the words of her very own second grade teacher, here was yet another door closed in Mandi's face...

TESTIMONY FROM MANDI'S THIRD GRADE TEACHER

Alice Mead* was deposed on May 31, 2001 at 1:56 p.m. She has worked for the Jefferson School Department for fifteen years as a third grade teacher at East Jefferson Elementary School. Like the rest of Mandi's teachers, Mrs. Mead is eager to paint a picture of Mandi as a good, but troubled, student:

Q: How would you characterize Mandi as a student?

A: Probably the thing that comes most to mind is difficulty interacting with peers and being very aware of what — or trying to be aware of what was going on around her while I was teaching.

I recall she was seated in the front row most of the time, possibly — often due to trying to keep her focused and keep her attention on what was going on. And what I do remember is that she was often turned around trying to see what may be going on around her, which was probably nothing because I was teaching at the time.

Q: And was there a conversation — who was there at that time, was it Mandi's mom?

A: Her report to me was that she was having a great deal of difficulty with Mandi at home, and she was not sure what to do about it. And my suggestion was that perhaps they should seek counseling for the family. It was not a school issue. It was a home issue with mother saying, "I'm not sure what to do." And the reason I remember this is because in my own family, probably two weeks earlier my own son had started counseling. And I saw what a benefit it could be for a child who needed it.

Q: So with regard to any incidents involving allegations of

harassment of Mandi, you were not aware of any such incidents?
A: No. No. I will say she had difficulty getting along with children.
And there were two girls in particular who were very best friends
that she wanted — she wanted to be friends with one of them. And
that was a focus for her, was to try to be a friend of the one.

These two girls, you have to understand, were very close. And I
think the way in which she tried to befriend one of them was not
appropriate. She really wanted to be a part of that, but probably
without that other girl involved. And neither of the girls wanted a
part of that.

Again, Charles Sylvester is amazingly effective at eliciting from
Mandi's teachers, almost to a one, that none of them had "any idea
of the ongoing incidents" at the bus stop, on the bus, in the hallways,
at recess, in the cafeteria, etc. Without accusation or incident, without
casting blame or even doubt, the Weins' lawyer has succeeded in
developing a pattern bordering on neglect, and emphasizing a line
straight from Hogan's Heroes Sergeant Schultz: "I see *nothing*, I
know *nothing!*"

Unlike a TV sit-com, however, the indifference and bad eyesight,
not to mention hearing, of Mandi's teachers had long-lasting and
damaging results to a third grader who just wanted to feel safe in the
classrooms of her elementary school.

Unfortunately, Mandi's torture did not stop in third grade...

TESTIMONY FROM MANDI'S FOURTH GRADE TEACHER

Debra Scone* was deposed on June 5, 2001 at 1:39 p.m. She has
worked for the Jefferson School Department for twenty-nine years
as a fourth grade teacher, all of them at East Jefferson Elementary
School.

As fourth grade was the last school year Mandi attended at East
Jefferson, the testimony of her fourth grade teacher is crucial to
Sylvester's case. Reading the testimony of all of Mandi's teachers,

one finds themselves crying out, "How could this have gone on for four long years? How could nobody have helped her? Did anybody care about this poor child, or just saving their butts?"

Unfortunately, there is no happy ending for Mandi Wein at East Jefferson. No one steps forth to save her. No one takes her hand and leads her to the principal's office to "get to the bottom of this." If anything, Sylvester makes it clear that Mandi is an outcast at East Jefferson, as evidenced in the following testimony:

Q: Now, during that parent/teacher conference did Mandi's mom make any complaints that Mandi had been bothered or harassed by any of her fellow students here at East Jefferson Elementary School at the bus stop, on the bus, or here at the school?

A: *I don't usually discuss things that happen outside of my classroom that I don't have purview over.* I maintain any discussions just on the classroom activity. So she may have said something about it then, but it was so long ago, I don't remember exactly what it was.

Q: And [you gave her] a grade 3 for Participates With Others, which is fair, is that true?

A: Yes.

Q: And what was the basis for those grades?

A: Well, conduct is how she comports herself in class. And participates with others, she was having difficulty getting along with other students.

I had been told by the principal that there had been some problems that the mother had said, you know, with certain individuals. So I worked at keeping those — her away from those individuals. I put her on one side of the room, the other students on the other. And I told them both to stay away from each other.

On many occasions she would follow those students around and bother them and annoy them, saying things as she passed by when she didn't have a reason to pass by them. She kept following them to the point where the kids would come to me — because I warned them. I said, "You stay away from her. And if she comes near you, you tell me." And they kept — they ran over to me on several occasions saying, "She keeps following us. We can't get away from her."

Q: Are they boys or girls that you're referring to?

A: These are girls.

Q: Did you separate any boys from her?

A: Basically, there was one boy I had to separate from everyone.

Q: Why was that?

A: He would harass other students. He would throw things at other students. He would get in their faces. I mean, right up close to them and challenge them. And — but he was an equal opportunity harasser. He would seek out certain people and he would do that, but it wasn't anyone on a particular day. He would choose somebody different every day.

Q: And this student — let me ask you this. Do you have in the classroom there in the fourth grade children who are deemed to be behaviorally disordered or emotionally disturbed for purposes of special education here at the East Jefferson Elementary School?

A: Yes, we do.

Q: And did this particular boy you're talking about, did he fall into one of those categories?

A: Yes, he does, and was later taken and put into Special Ed class.

Q: Do you recall an incident that occurred at recess involving Mandi?

A: No, because I kept Mandi next to me. I said to her that in order to keep her safe and the other children wouldn't pick on her, she could stand by me and keep me company.

Q: Do you recall Mandi coming to you and making a complaint to you that children in the class were calling her names and threatening to beat her up?

A: Yes, I do.

Q: And when did that occur?

A: I have no idea. I remember speaking with her about it. Do I remember whether it happened the beginning of September, the end of September, October, I —

Q: Now, and is that — what did you do in response to that complaint that Mandi made to you?

A: I went to the children that she had said had committed the offense and spoke to them and first I asked what happened, because in any situation many times I find six of one, half of another. So I have to sort it out, who said what, what was said, who actually said it.

Q: With regard to this incident, do you have a recollection that you actually spoke to the other children that Mandi said were threatening her and calling her names?

A: I remember speaking to the students. I remember sitting them down and talking to them. The specifics of any one particular incident, I don't know.

Q: Did it happen —

A: You know, it wasn't yesterday. You know, it happened a long time ago. This is the way I handle it. I know I talked to those students. I know I told them to stay away from her. I know I told them they would lose recess if I caught them anywhere near her. And vice versa, the same thing with her.

Q: You know —

A: She needs to stay away from them too.

Q: And when you separated the children in the classroom, as you testified before, did you do that of your own volition or were you directed to do that by Mr. Larcon?

A: I did that on my own.

Q: So he did not direct you to separate the children in the classroom; is that true?

A: That's true.

Despite the subtleties of legalese, there are several things that quickly become evident as Mandi's fourth grade teacher is deposed. First, she is well-versed in the company line, as evidenced by her statement: "I don't usually discuss things that happen outside of my classroom that I don't have purview over."

Naturally. Why look past your classroom door when it's not a part of your job description? Why do more than you're required? Furthermore, however, Sylvester goes on to make the point that Mrs. Scone not only didn't care much for Mandi, "She kept following them to the point where the kids would come to me — because I warned them. I said, 'You stay away from her. And if she comes near you, you tell me,'" but also wasn't too fond of Mr. Sylvester, either "You know, it wasn't yesterday. You know, it happened a long time ago."

Although, to her credit, Mrs. Scone says that she kept Mandi by her side "to protect her," her above words to the students sound more like a conspiracy than concern. It should be noted that Mrs. Scone has been teaching for close to thirty years. Had a first year teacher, perhaps, or even one with just shy of a decade under their belt, handled things so inappropriately, it might have been more excusable.

But a veteran should obviously know better...

Lastly, however, Mrs. Scone's words conclude with finality that anything she did as a teacher she did on her own. Mr. Larcon, Mandi's principal at the time, did not order her to separate any of her students. Did not ask her how Mandi was doing. Did not check up on Mandi, or detain any of her students, or even Mandi for that matter.

The questions remains obvious as her testimony ends: What, if anything, did Mandi's principal do?

TESTIMONY FROM MANDI'S FIRST PRINCIPAL

No longer an employee of the Jefferson School Department, Mandi's former principal Marcus Washington had little to add to the proceedings, short of the following exchange:

Q: Please state in complete detail any and all conversations you had with Mandi Passarelli, Mark Passarelli, or Debra Wein, including but not limited to the incidents set forth in the complaint.

A: I do not recall specific conversations with Mandi, Mark Passarelli, or Debra Wein. As a student and parents in the school, I am sure there were some interactions, however, I do not recall any specific ones.

Thanks to his lack of testimony and/or input in these proceedings, Dr. Washington becomes an enigma. Not only does his silence speak on behalf of his own negligence, but that of the entire East Jefferson School district.

TESTIMONY FROM MANDI'S SECOND PRINCIPAL

Dennis Larcon* is deposed on May 4, 2001 at 10:00 a.m. Holding a principal's certificate issued by the State of Rhode Island, he also has a lifetime teaching certificate for elementary grades and middle school, as well as an endorsement for English as a second language. He has worked for the Jefferson School Department for two and a half years, all of them at East Jefferson Elementary School.

Unfortunately for Dennis Larcon, the brunt of the blame for what has happened to Mandi Wein has fallen on him. Though he was only her principal for less than a year, Mr. Washington's absence in both these legal proceedings and the school district put Larcon squarely on the hot seat where, as you will shortly see from his bumbling answers, he feels far from comfortable:

Q: When you say that [Mandi] complained that the same fifth grade student was beginning to call her names on the bus and pushing her, how do you know that? Was that a conversation you had with her, or was it a conversation she had with a teacher?

A: Because Mandi probably came to me and told me what happened.

Q: When you use the word probably, it makes me suspect that you're speculating. So I'm asking you — there's a difference between what you actually recollect — you may not recall.

A: I can't be totally clear. I can't be totally clear. I can only say that a child comes to my office through a teacher with a complaint, and I bring the child in and talk to the child about what happened.

Q: And you know the identity of the fifth grade student that you're referring to…is that correct?

A: Yes.

Q: But you don't — correct me if I'm wrong, you don't recall the exact details of that conversation with Mandi?

A: Not at that initial, no, I don't.

Q: And what exactly did she say? What did she say the child was doing?

A: Calling her names at the bus stop and on the bus.

Q: And pushing her; is that correct?

A: And pushing, yes.

Q: Now, it says 'I questioned the student and she admitted it.'

A: Yes.

Q: And that's the fifth grade student that you're referring to?

A: Yes.

Q: And where did you question the student?

A: In my office.

Q: And what was the conversation you had with the student?

A: Basically what it is is did you push Mandi, did you call her names and push her. And the girl said yes, I did.

Q: And what words did she say that she used?

A: I can't recall exact words.

Q: Do you recall the words that Mandi said that the girl used when she was called names?

A: What words was she called?

Q: Yes.

A: I can't recollect that either.

Q: On any occasion do you recall whether or not you received any complaints of Mandi Passarelli had been the subject of any sexual epithets or expletives or words of that nature?

A: No. I was never informed of any.

Q: And what types of names were you aware that she had been called?

A: A bitch. A fat bitch.

Q: I know some of these words are unpleasant.

A: No, it's all right. I hear a lot of them in school. Ass. Asshole. Those types of things.

Q: And did you have a conversation with Detective Jaffi from the Jefferson Police Department?

A: Yes, I did.

Q: And what was said during the course of that conversation?

A: I don't recall the whole conversation. He did say that he just came back from Mrs. Wein's house, and she was upset about problems happening at the bus and at the bus stop. I told him we're doing what we can here to take care of these issues. She made the decision that she would go to the police and file a complaint of some kind, and Detective Jaffi, like juvenile officers do, they come into the school and check in and find out the basis of the complaint and what's going on at the school.

Q: What type of a student was Mandi Passarelli?

A: Well, I felt that she was part of the problem. She was a major part of this problem here.

Q: Why do you say that?

A: Because I feel that her behavior warranted these actions that she did with other children. I don't feel that she was — I feel that she was a major part of the problem.

Q: Could you read back the last response please?

[ANSWER READ BACK BY COURT REPORTER]

Q: You said just then that her behavior warranted these actions. What do you mean by that?

A: I meant that her behavior and her relationship with other children, these are the actions that came out of it was the hitting, the pushing, the shoving.

Q: You're not saying that any pushing or shoving of her was warranted based on her behavior?

A: I'm saying that if — that a child would push her or swear at her because she had just done the same thing to that child.

Q: Now, did you observe that?

A: No, I didn't.

Q: So, when you say that, you're not basing any of that on personal knowledge; is that true?

A: No. I'm going by from what the children would tell me.

Though buried in his short and clipped answers, Larcon's responses to Sylvester's questions are nonetheless chilling. Here is a man charged with running an entire school. Not a huge school, with 7,000 students, not even a big school, with 1,700 students, but a relatively small school of 700 students. While it is easy to armchair principal and throw stones at glass houses, one would assume Larcon is not alone in his dealings with the students.

From teachers to secretaries to nurses to other support staff, his load is lightened and work is delegated. And yet he can barely "recall" many of the incidents in which Mandi was involved that year, if any.

And his main source of evidence for those instances which he does remember? "I'm going by from what the children would tell me." Above and beyond his apparent aloofness from his 700 students however, his lack of action on punishing Mandi's attackers speaks volumes.

No expulsions, no suspensions, a couple of detentions, maybe, a parent meeting or two, and that is it. What kind of message is that sending? A loud one, if you're listening that is. And if there's one things students *do* listen to, it's the unspoken words of their elders.

The bottom line in Mr. Larcon's administration, according to the Weins and in fact the above testimony, was that if you picked on Mandi Wein, you could easily get away with it.

More chilling, however, is the one comment in all of this testimony that Charles Sylvester deems fit to re-read back into the record: "Because I feel that her behavior warranted these actions that she did with other children. I don't feel that she was — I feel that she was a major part of the problem."

For once, even a restrained and conservative Sylvester can barely hide his repulsion: "You're not saying that any pushing or shoving of her was warranted based on her behavior?"

Unfortunately for Mr. Larcon, and the school district of Jefferson

County, the damage had already been done.

Just ask Mandi Wein...

TESTIMONY FROM THE SCHOOL SUPERINTENDENT

Phillip Mackey* is deposed on April 30, 2001 at 2:00 p.m. He is the superintendent of the Jefferson County School Board, and as such the one, final place where, indeed, the buck does stop. Unfortunately, even his testimony reveals that he is even *more* in the dark than any of the secretaries, nurses, teachers, and principals that have testified before him:

Q: Do you know if you have ever received any incident reports relating to Mandi Passarelli?

A: I'm not sure.

Q: Did you review any recourse, such as that general file, to determine whether there are in fact any incident reports relating to Mandi Passarelli?

B: I'm not sure.

Q: So it's safe to say before coming here today you did not look in that general file where you kept incident reports, correct?

A: Correct.

Q: You have been the superintendent of the Jefferson School Department since May of 1999, true?

A: Yes.

Q: Have you received complaints of sexual harassment since May of '99?

A: No, not that I can recall.

Q: So am I correct in saying that there is no central location that you're aware of, since you received no complaints since May of '99, you don't have a file for all sexual harassment complaints?

A: I've had no occasion to refer to a file if there is a file.

Q: My questions — I know you reviewed that report prior to coming here today. And my question is when did you first review that police report?

A: This was — what's the date on this?

Q: The date of the report that you're looking at at the top says October 14, 1999. And it relates to a phone complaint made by Debra Wein, Mandi Passarelli's mother. And I'm simply asking you whether you had, prior to this litigation, reviewed that police report? Had anyone showed you the police report?

A: No, not to my knowledge.

Q: Has anyone contacted you from the Jefferson Police Department with regard to a phone complaint made by Debra Wein relating to harassment of her daughter?

A: No, not to my knowledge.

Q: And similarly, with regard to the police report that is dated November the 12th of 1999, which is another phone complaint to the Jefferson Police Department from Debra Wein regarding a complaint of assault, when did you first see that document, Doctor?

A: I don't think I saw it prior to the —

Q: The lawsuit being filed?

A: — the lawsuit.

Q: Now, were you ever contacted by anyone from the Jefferson Police Department with regard to complaints that had been made to the Jefferson Police Department regarding harassment or assaults on Mandi Passarelli?

A: Not to my knowledge.

Q: So you never talked to Detective Jaffi or any of these detectives with regard to any such complaint; is that correct?

A: That's correct.

Q: You had conversations with Mr. Larcon [Mandi's principal] about what he did to deal with any complaints of harassment of Mandi Passarelli; is that correct?

A: Prior to the complaint?

Q: I'm talking about actions that he may have taken in response to any allegations of harassment of Mandi Passarelli. My question to you is did you ever ask him what he did in response to such complaints?

A: Yes.

Q: What did he tell you?

A: He told me that he responded to each of those complaints, implementing the policy, as he has done with any student who comes forward with a complaint, as well as a parent. He deals with it as a school principal. He's had complaints about problems at the bus stop that he's dealt with, recess at school. He's invoked —

Q: With regard to this particular student, Mandi Passarelli?

A: Yes. He's invoked suspension, I believe, over a student or two as a result of Mandi's interaction with other students.

Q: Your records reveal that students at the — in the Jefferson School Department have been suspended as a result of allegations of harassment of Mandi Passarelli?

A: I believe what I read in Mr. Larcon's interrogatories as that an interaction between her and a male student, I believe he suspend the male student of or one day. That was an allegation of using a vulgarity. I can find that for you.

Q: Without reviewing his answers in detail, he indicates, "I sent a boy home for one day"?

A: Right.

Q: So other than that — that's what you were referring to?

A: Other than what I read here, I don't know of any other interactions that Mr. Larcon has had with Mandi.

Q: With regard to Mr. Washington [Mandi's former principal] did you have any conversations with Mr. Washington after the lawsuit was filed?

A: My only conversation with Mr. Washington was to inform him of the complaint when we received the complaint.

Q: Is he teaching in a different district now?

A: Yes. I don't know Mr. Washington personally. I just called to inform him of the complaint.

Q: And what did he say?

A: We basically didn't really have a conversation; just let him know there was a complaint and that he had vaguely, vaguely had some memory of the student, but not the specifics.

Q: Doctor, I'm going to ask you to identify, if you haven't already, every document that is in the possession of the Jefferson School Department that relates to any complaints of harassment of abuse of Mandi Passarelli.

A: I'm just trying to recall. Outside of seeing Mr. Sylvester's letter and the two police reports, I can't recall any other one. I can't recall any other document.

Q: You're not aware of any witness statements of statement taken from any individuals with regard to any complaints of harassment of Mandi Passarelli; is that correct?

A: That's correct.

Q: Now, without identifying any children personally, do you know the names of any of the children who were involved with any of these incidents that are set forth in the complaint?

A: No, I do not.

Q: So you have never spoken to any of the children; is that correct?

A: No. That's correct.

Q: And you have never presided over any sort of disciplinary hearings with regard to any children regarding incidents involving Mandi Passarelli; is that correct?

A: That's correct.

It's not so much what Mackey did, as what he *didn't* do. No recognition of the names of the children involved. No meetings with any of the parents. No meetings with *Mandi's* parents. Not even a meeting with either Dr. Washington or Dr. Larcon, Mandi's own principals.

Why, he couldn't even be bothered to read Mandi's file before he testified!

Naturally, school superintendents can't be bothered with every single triviality that crosses their desks. If the principals at Mandi's school couldn't keep track of just one of their students in a sea of 700, imagine the sheer numbers Mr. Mackey was dealing with. It is understandable that he might not be privy to every insult, epithet, or hair-pulling incident poor Mandi endured.

But the Weins' lawsuit was no sudden surprise to the Jefferson County School Board. It certainly wasn't sprung on them the day before he testified for Mr. Sylvester and the Rhode Island federal courts. He wasn't blind-sided, by any means. The fact that he spoke with Dr. Washington prior to testifying was obviously an attempt to ramp up to speed to prevent a trial.

But in even that, Mackey and the rest of the Jefferson County School Board failed. With even the brief excerpts posted here, in order of appearance, it becomes quite clear that one pattern emerges within all of this testimony: Nobody did anything.

Nobody helped. Nobody had any meetings, conferences, calls, or strategy sessions beyond the run-of-the-mill parent conference. Or a single trip to the bus stop. Or a meeting about "the stick incident," and only because "the boy's parents" were upset!

Though no one calls Mandi any names or disparages her parents in any way, the feeling is nonetheless clear in the litany of proceeding testimony: "Mandi and her parents were a nag, troublemakers that made us all look bad. Now we've been caught with our pants down, if we just stick to the story that she was the problem, that she was at fault, we'll get through this okay."

Certainly, hindsight is 20/20. Even if some of these teachers and other educational professionals had admitted their mistakes, the stakes might have changed. Or if policy was changed. If a single one of them had said, "I pay more attention to my trouble students now," or even something even vaguely resembling that response.

Unfortunately, towing the company line and sticking to the story leaves you unable to do one important thing: show remorse.

But now it was the parents' turn...

MARK'S TESTIMONY

Mark Joseph Passarelli was deposed on Thursday, May 10, 2001 at 4:40 p.m. He is Mandi's father, and the gist of his testimony is quite simple: The school wouldn't help, so I tried to take matters into my own hands. Unfortunately, that didn't work either:

Q: Just to back up a little bit. I'm going to go back, I know I got a lot of history from your wife. So I'm not going to go over it again. I do want to ask you when Mandi was being bothered on the daily basis, for instance, in the first grade at the bus stop, what did you do, if anything?

A: Actually, a lot of the times, sometimes I was home, sometimes I wasn't, but when I did find out I chose to take the appropriate action and do things the right way and start with the parents and I spoke to the parents.

Q: And this would be the three boys?

A: Yes.

Q: This is Skeeter?

A: Yes.

Q: Pugsley and —

A: And Rizzo I think.

Q: And Rizzo?

A: Yup.

Q: That's the house around the corner?

A: Up the street, yeah.

Q: And you went to see the parents?

A: Yes, the father. There's no mother.

Q: Would this be in the first part of the year?

A: Of first grade.

Q: Of first grade?

A: Yes, I believe so.

Q: And what, if anything, happened as a result — did you actually—

A: I actually physically went and talked to the father.

Q: What happened?

A: Nothing, he was very rude but nothing happened.

Q: Did you tell him that the kids were bothering your daughter?

A: Of course.

Q: And he didn't say anything about it?

A: "I'll have him stop."

Q: And did you speak to Dennis Larcon?

A: Yes.

Q: When did you speak to Dennis Larcon?

A: October of '99.

Q: Tell us about that conversation.

A: I called him up, my wife, again my wife had a difficult time trying to get him to do anything, so I called and I asked him, I told him what was going on and I asked him if it could stop and he got very rude with me and he started yelling at me and then when he yelled at me I yelled back and, you know, this is my little girl, my daughter, and I was very concerned and I was very irate and that's what happened.

Q: Well, could you tell me what actually substantively, I know you got upset, he got upset and everybody yelled at each other.

A: What really got me upset was he said he had seven hundred kids to take care of — he said I have seven hundred kids to take care of, I can't just take care of your kid. That was his exact words.

Q: And other than speaking to Skeeter's dad, did you speak to any other parents?

A: I went to the bottom of the street to some girl, I forgot her name, Tiara, yea, I spoke to her mom, too.

Q: And this was in '99, right?

A: '99.

Q: That's when you got a note?

A: Late afternoon.

Q: What did you and Mrs./ the mother of Tiara, discuss?

A: Basically that I wanted her to stop. My daughter was on the bus an she took, she said she took a hairpiece from my daughter and I wasn't home at the time and when I got home I guess my oldest daughter was home, my wife wasn't home and what had happens is she chased Mandi home to the door. She wanted money, fifty cents, for a hairpiece that Mandi had sat on I guess and she was bullying her and it was just continuous and then I went, when I got home, down to the end of the street and asked the mother to have it stopped...

Q: And what did the mother say?
A: Nothing, she never stopped it.

Mark's testimony makes it clear that he was a concerned father, but by his own admission, "sometimes I was home, sometimes I wasn't." And though his attempts to rectify his daughter's perilous predicament were admirable, they also reveal his inner turmoil and mounting frustration.

Like Mandi, like Debra, Mark, too, was powerless in the face of an uncaring and inefficient bureaucracy that let his entire family down...

DEBRA'S TESTIMONY

Debra Lynn Wein was deposed on Thursday, May 10, 2001 at 2:00 p.m. She is Mandi's mother. Debra Wein's strategy for solving Mandi's problems was quite different, but, alas, no more effective. At every turn, she tries to find a solution, a recourse, that will stop Mandi's torturous abuse. She asks teachers, all of them, she asks principals, both of them, she asks the school board, and, finally, she asks the local police. For all of her effort, her pleas quite obviously fell on deaf ears:

Q: It would be a fair statement to say that this harassment took place on a daily basis.
A: Pretty much so, yeah.
Q: And it would be daily?
A: Yes.
Q: Mandi would complain to you each and every day, basically?
A: Yes, she did.
Q: And so she would be harassed at the bus stop?
A: Correct.
Q: She'd be harassed in the...recess yard daily?
A: Right.

Q: Now, as a result of the first one or two incidents I presume you notified the authorities at the school.

A: Yes, I did.

Q: Now, as I understand it...each quarter you would have a parent/teacher conference?

A: I don't remember if it was after each quarter or if there was just two meetings.

Q: Suffice it to say you would have a formal meeting, that's standard operating procedure, isn't it?

A: Right.

Q: And I presume during those meetings, of course, one of your main subjects to Mrs. Frank [Mandi's first grade teacher] would be the fact that Mandi on a daily basis is being harassed at the bus stop and during recess?

A: I'd mentioned it to her but that wasn't her area, it was the principal.

Q: My question is very narrow. I'm asking you as her teacher you would've told her, would you not that on a daily basis Mandi is being harassed both at the bus stop and during recess?

A: Yes, I did, but once these told me that that was something that I have to speak with the principal about, unless it actually was someone from her class that was bothering her.

Q: So I take it these six to ten individuals who were bothering her throughout that academic year, the nine months, were not in her class?

A: No, they were not.

Q: So as I understand it you complained to Mrs. Frank that this was going on on a daily basis and she said they're not my students, it's not my problem, call the principal?

A: She said, you know, she basically can't discipline, I guess, kids in other grades, that's the principal's job.

Q: Well, I presume, you know, your daughter comes home from school the first two or three weeks and these kid are harassing her and you've very concerned.

A: Exactly.

Q: And, therefore, you're going to try to do something about it, aren't you?

A: Right.

Q: So when that happened the first time, did you immediately call her teacher or did you immediately call Mr. Washington [Mandi's then principal]?

A: I immediately called Dr. Washington.

Q: And how many times did you speak to Mr. Washington, for instance, in the period September '96 through December '96?

A: I would speak to him at that time probably three times a week.

Q: Three times a week?

A: I would call him three times a week.

Q: You call him three times a week and how many times would you speak to him?

A: At least twice.

Q: And would you speak to him twice a week for the period from January '97 to June '97?

A: Yes.

Q: And according to the complaint as I read it, he absolutely did nothing for you.

A: He explained to me that three of the boys came from a very bad family, you know, they were going through a lot of hard times being raised by a single parent. One of them was on medication, and he would talk to the father and see what he could do.

Q: Did you ever observe any of these incidents which are the subject of the complaint here?

A: Yes.

Q: What did you observe?

A: Three boys, the three boys from that one house, calling Mandi filthy, rotten names.

Q: And when you heard that, I presume you went to the bus stop and told them to stop?

A: I, you know, I'm a house away. When they — before they called her the names they pushed her, then as she was going against the stairway they called her the names, and I told them "Leave her alone, go play with the boys, she's a little girl."

Q: When did you start driving [Mandi to school]?

A: November [of '96].

Q: So what was the date that you hurt yourself?

A: March of '97.

Q: And I presume as the result of your fall in '97, you weren't able to drive?

A: Correct.

Q: Now, as I understand it, in reviewing your answers to interrogatories for grade 2, it was once again a continuous harassment at the bus stop and during recess.

A: Correct.

Q: And this took place for the school year '97 through '98?

A: Correct.

Q: And it was on a daily basis?

A: Oh, yeah.

Q: And would it be fair to say that once again you would speak to Mr. Washington twice a week during this period?

A: It was probably a little more at that time.

Q: So it was two or more times per week every week for 1997 through 1998?

A: Correct.

Q: And no results.

A: Never.

In the preceding testimony, Sylvester carefully takes Debra through Mandi's ongoing torment. While none of the information is new or startling in itself, the breadth of the Weins' complaint is staggering, especially in light of the "know nothing, see nothing" testimony of the educational professionals preceding it: Four years. Two calls a week. And still no one can recall a single complaint, a single time when Mandi was in the right, when it wasn't, at least partially, *her* fault!

But the Weins' case isn't simply about finding fault or laying blame. Far from it. Their contention is and always has been that the abuse suffered at East Jefferson Elementary School, for four long years, had both lasting and costly affects on Mandi's fragile personality.

Here Sylvester carefully plants the seeds of what life was like at the Wein home in between torturous school years, and later how the experience affected Mandi's very ability to leave the house or socialize with old friends:

Q: And what would be her activities during the summer between the second and third grade?

A: Like I said, she spent a lot of time with her sisters. We would go for rides, we would go to the beach, a lot of family time.

Q: And once again during the summers, the summer between second and third grade, did she have any friends, a little friend, other than family?

A: A lot of her friends went to camp and she did not want to go, so...

Q: What's her reasons for not going to camp?

A: She said no one will bother me if I stay home.

Q: And she felt that if she went to camp, once again, there would be problems?

A: Right.

Q: Now, the third grade, she starts in September of '98; is that right?

A: Right.

Q: And that year, once again, throughout the academic year September '97, through June — September '98, through June of '99, it was the same old thing?

A: Same old.

Q: Every day?

A: Yup.

Q: At the bus stop, is that correct?

A: Chased home from the bus stop.

Q: She was harassed at the bus stop?

A: Yes.

Q: She's harassed on the bus?

A: Yes.

Q: And she's harassed at recess?

A: Correct.

Q: And this occurred on a daily basis?

A: Yes.

Q: Now, did [Mandi's new principal] Mr. Larcon give you any satisfaction concerning curtailing these activities?

A: No.

Q: Did he ever go to the bus stop, Mr. Larcon?

A: He went once.

Q: And what happened when he went to the bus stop?

A: He parked in front of my house, he got out of the car and he stood there and was talking to me. I was standing on the porch and no one bothered Mandi that day. They're not going to do it right in front of the principal either.

Q: Were any students in her class participating in this harassing activity in the third grade?

A: No.

Q: None. And would it be — how many students were participating in this harassing activity?

A: There were two more this year.

Q: So how many do we have altogether?

A: Maybe ten to twelve?

Q: And were names reported to Mr. Larcon?

A: Yes, they were.

Q: Now, between the third and fourth grade summers, what would Mandi's activities encompass?

A: Mandi at that time, it was the same, same thing every summer, basically a lotta family time, a lotta day trips.

Q: And did she have any friends that would visit with her during the summer?

A: Mandi? No, no. Mandi stopped liking people at that time.

Q: Between the third and fourth grade you say that she didn't want people to visit because she didn't like them.

A: She didn't want people around her, she didn't even like going out.

Q: Now, she begins school in the fourth grade with Mrs. Scone, and that's in September of '99, is that right?

A: Correct.

Q: And was it once again she was daily abused?

A: First day of school.

Q: And that would be September through then you removed her, November...18th?

A: Something like that.

Q: The first day to November 18, '99, and it was daily that she was bothered?

A: Oh, yeah.

Q: Now, you removed her from the Jefferson system in November of '99.

A: Correct.

Q: And when did she start at the Hebrew Day?

A: I don't remember the exact date.

Q: And did she start as a fourth grade student?

A: Yes, she did.

Q: And she passed the fourth grade.

A: Oh, yeah.

Q: And she was happy?

A: I wouldn't say happy.

Q: Why wouldn't you say happy?

A: Mandi's been very sad since everything happened. I mean, just because she changed schools scholastically is totally different than her every day mental status.

Q: Now, September 2000, she starts in fifth grade.

A: Correct.

Q: Between September 2000, and December 2000, she have any disciplinary problems?

A: Yes, she did.

Q: And what were those?

A: She started stealing food.

Q: And what was the explanation as to why she was stealing food?

A: She was, she had to, she just had to. Mandi has obsessive compulsive disorder and it was an obsession for her, a compulsion for her.

Q: Did she complete the fifth grade there?

A: No she didn't.

Q: Why not?

A: She was asked to leave the school because they are not equipped to handle her problems.

Q: And what problems weren't they equipped to handle?

A: The obsessive compulsive disorder, the depression and PTSD, post traumatic stress disorder.

Q: So when, approximately, did she leave the fifth grade at Hebrew Day?

A: Right before Christmas break.

Q: That would be in December of 2000. And did you attempt to put her into alternative learning?

A: Mandi goes to tutoring now.

Q: Who tutors her?

A: It's through the Jefferson schools.

Q: And does she physically go someplace?

A: She goes to the administration building.

Q: And she goes there every day?

A: No, she goes for six hours a week.

Q: And who is her tutor there?

A: Elizabeth Byerly.

In the preceding testimony, Sylvester does an efficient lengthy job of picturing an older, more troubled, less mainstream Mandi. Still, his contention is clear: Before the abuse started, Mandi was a shy but friendly, cute but talkative little girl. After the abuse, she was a troubled child who became not only compulsive but unable to function in a "normal" school setting.

A "special student" who must now be tutored at the school board building! And, while little "evidence" supported Mandi's ongoing abuse at East Jefferson, the evidence present in her aftermath is nearly overwhelming: fear of summer camp, the mall, and other trips with her family, a compulsion to eat, to steal food, and an increasingly erratic and unstable home life that her mother contends was never a problem before. As the questioning finally concludes, Sylvester wants to hammer home one last, touching point of Mandi's life, before and after:

Q: Has Mandi done anything unusual in your eyes in the last six months that you found to be abnormal?

A: She's done a lot.

Q: Tell me, give me an example.

A: I'm trying to think. She's constantly, since Mandi you know, since we've gotten her diagnosis and everything, she gets very, very depressed and food has become her very, best friend and she's just constantly, you know, wanting to eat and, you know, we tell her, you have to lose a little bit of weight and it's not healthy. Mandi can be very, very difficult, very argumentative, and this is not my Mandi. You know, I want to tell you that Mandi before all this happened was a very happy child. She was social and bubbly and she was just a great person to be around, and now she's just very sad and somber and she gets very angry, why am I like this, why can't I be a normal kid, and why can't I go do this and why can't I do that, and I'm going to be taking these retard pills for all my life, and she gets very mad and very depressed over this.

The point both Mr. Sylvester and Debra are trying to make is very clear: That was then, this is *now*...

FOR THE CHILDREN ...
Putting a Stop to Schoolyard Abuse

WHAT CAN YOUR CHILD DO TO AVOID BEING BULLIED?

Being bullied is *never* your child's fault, and they should never be blamed for falling prey to a schoolyard bully. However, there are a few simple things your child can do to decrease the risk that they maybe be bullied:

Act confident: your child could do this by holding his head up as he walks. Teach him to imagine walking tall and to look people in the eye.

Make a point of finding friends: ask other children over to your house, join sports or organized clubs where your child will meet others interested in the same things.

Hang around with friends: when adults are not around your child and her friends should stick together. A bully probably won't approach your child when she's in a group.

When you tell your child you love him, respect him and when you listen to him you build up his confidence, self-esteem and trust in you. These are their best weapons to deal with any bullies your child may meet.

CHAPTER ELEVEN:
The Verdict

As the long, hot summer of 2001 winds down and the rest of East Jefferson's children prepare to go back to school, Mandi Wein has little too look forward to. Numbed by the anti-depressants and other prescriptions her doctor has ordered for her ongoing treatment for post-traumatic stress disorder, PTSD and obsessive compulsive disorder, or OCD, the modern Mandi Wein is a shell of herself.

Ornery and irritable at home, the approaching fall is yet another reminder that she is an outcast, a "special student," an outsider. Even her family, her loyal, loving family finds it hard to contend with Mandi's mood swings and eating disorder, and despite their ongoing family counseling she knows that they have a long road ahead of them before they are ever fully "recovered" from the incident that has interrupted, if not totally destroyed, her life.

But, still, fall brings with it as much good news as it does bad, at least in the hallowed halls of The United States District Court for the District of Rhode Island in the US Federal Building and Courthouse.

At long last, the testimony of all those involved was over, and the Weins were back in court. But not for long. Instead of going to trial, the powers that be in the Jefferson County School Board, while not conceding guilt, of course, offer the Weins and their lawyer, Charles Sylvester, an undisclosed sum that is purportedly in the six figure realm.

Mark and Debra are stunned, their lawyer is pleased, if not exactly happy, and practically before it started the whole, sordid affair is over.

The trial of the Weins vs. the Town of Jefferson was narrowly averted when lawyers for the Jefferson County School Board decided to settle with the Weins before a costly — and potentially damaging — jury trial was set to begin. Though lawyers for the school board downplay *which* of the six figures the court awarded the Weins, one thing is clear: Culpability was proven in a case that never went to court.

But "winning" is a word the Weins would never use to describe their verdict in the case of their daughter versus the school board. Scorned by their community, threatened at home, parents of a daughter forever scarred by her experiences in the Jefferson County School System, the Weins are reluctant heroes to a small but loyal community of educators devoted to seeing safe schools — and children safe at school.

And, after the dust settles and the courtroom clears and her lawyer leaves to collect their check from the Jefferson County School Board, Debra can't help but feel that the ending is just a bit more than anti-climactic.

After all, they've risked their life savings on a trial lawyer, the scorn of their town for revealing the truth, and the very sanity of their little girl as they put her through the rigors of testifying in her very own defense.

A necessary, if costly, evil.

And as she prepares to address the handful of reporters waiting for her reaction to the verdict, Debra is hard pressed for what to say. Should she thank her lawyer, for finally revealing the truth? Should she thank Mandi, for enduring her abuse for four long years? Should she thank the school board, for finally coming to their senses?

In the end, of course, there are no winners in a case like this. Debra Wein knows this more than perhaps anyone else in the courtroom that day. After all, the judge was not there to see Mandi's bruises, her tears, her pain. Her lawyer wasn't there to hear her daughter tossing and turning every school night, desperate to fall asleep but just as afraid of the nightmares that would come the minute she closed her eyes.

And the school board? Well, they were there, or at least their representatives were, but saw fit to ignore the problem, thinking it would all "just go away."

Perhaps, Debra thinks as she and Mark finally leave the courtroom to address the waiting reporters, *that's what will come out of this. We can't get those four years back for Mandi. The money we got won't put a dent in her medical bills over the next dozen or so years. The victory is hollow, the same teachers are still in the same classrooms at the same school.*

But, perhaps, the school board will think twice before ignoring another elementary, junior high, or even high school student who complains about verbal, physical, or sexual abuse.

Perhaps what Mandi went through won't be in vain if, because of her courage in coming forward and taking the Jefferson County School Board to court, another Mandi's abuse is stopped the minute it starts.

It's not much, she thinks, *but maybe it's enough...*

FOR THE CHILDREN ...
Putting a Stop to Schoolyard Abuse

WHAT TO DO IF...*YOUR* CHILD IS THE BULLY

At the opposite end of the spectrum, as much as parents do not want to hear that their child is being bullied at school, parents also do not want to hear that their child is, in fact, the bully! Upon hearing that your child is displaying bully behavior, it is best not to get defensive. Rather than discussing "why" he or she is a bully, try to find what is causing your child to behave in this manner. Take the time to sit down and talk with your child, and let him or her know the following:

Clearly inform your child that hurting people is not okay, and that bullying behaviors are not acceptable in your family, or society in general.

Define the consequences you will impose if the behavior continues.

Try role-playing. Discuss ways and come up with scenarios of how your child can deal with the situation without bullying other children.

Increase the time you spend together as a family.

Limit the amount of time your child watches or is exposed to violent messages in the media.

While teaching new behavior, reward more appropriate behaviors that the child displays.

CONCLUSION:
Justice for Mandi?

It should come as no surprise that Mandi Wein still bears the scars of her physical, verbal, emotional, and sexual abuse at the hands of ten to twelve students, not to mention the faculty, staff, and administration at East Jefferson Elementary.

According to Debra, she has her good days, she has her bad days. She fights with her sisters, but what middle sister doesn't? Still, the entire Wein family knows that Mandi's troubles run much deeper than that, and they fully support her ongoing treatment of counseling and medication.

She still dreads leaving the house, and has never fully socialized as other children her age with "normal" educational backgrounds might. Like a woman who has been raped or a businessman who's been mugged outside of his plush downtown office after working one too many a late night, Mandi will never, ever, be the same.

Her past still haunts her, and clouds her future with a stormy horizon. Mandi should be in the seventh grade by now. Unfortunately, her various behavioral problems and societal fears, both real and imagined, prevent her from attending regular classes with students her same age.

As Mandi approaches her teen years, and puberty, all Debra Wein can do is hope and pray that time will, indeed, heal all wounds. Still, she knows that is more of a pipe dream than a foreseeable reality.

A book such as this should have a happy ending and, while the admission of a guilt and a six-figure settlement from the East Jefferson School Board should have been just that, the Weins are left with a decidedly empty victory.

Mandi is still troubled, still popping pills, and still considered a "special student." Her troubles have no end in sight, and despite the fact that, ever the fighter, Debra Wein has learned everything there is to know — and more — about the disorders from which she suffers and the medications she is on, the Weins know that they face an uphill battle in the fight for Mandi's recovery.

Amazingly, the Weins still live in the same East Jefferson neighborhood. And, while Mandi is alternately home-schooled and tutored by the county who publicly admitted their negligence in her former education, both of her sisters attended local schools without incident.

They were the lucky ones...

Mark and Debra are still together, despite the emotional upheaval of Mandi's experience, the subsequent trial, and her ongoing behavioral problems and emotional acting out. They solve their problems they way they always have, as a family.

They plan to move to Florida as soon as their jobs and finances will allow. The surface reason is so that they can be closer to Debra's mother, but the entire family knows that mostly it is so that Mandi can get a new lease on life, in a new town, where no one knows her past.

No one knows her name...

As for the teachers, secretaries, nurses, principals, and school board members involved in this disturbing story, most of them are still in the positions they held at the time of Mandi's abuse.

Not surprisingly, as a result of the media attention both locally and nationally that resulted in the Wein's landmark legal battles and unprecedented settlement in this matter, other children have now had the courage to admit that they, too, were bullied, cursed, and even abused at the hands of the same students, in the same school, in the same school district.

Their cases, as is Mandi's future, are still pending...

FOR THE CHILDREN...
Other Books That Might Help

The following is a list of other books on the topic of playground justice and schoolyard bullying. Whether your child is being bullied, or the bully, whether you are a teacher or an administrator, education is perhaps the one way to effectively stop schoolyard abuse. It is hoped that these books, in addition to *Playground Justice,* can provide just that. They include:

And Words Can Hurt Forever: *How to Protect Adolescents from Bullying, Harassment, and Emotional Violence* by James Garbarino and Ellen deLara (**The Free Press**, 2002)

Despite the best intentions of school administrators, educators, and parents, many schools — even those that have addressed bullying and are considered safe — unwittingly support and enable hostile and threatening environments. As a society, we are only just beginning to understand the degree of damage that bullying inflicts on individual teenagers and on their relationships later in life. In this groundbreaking work, James Garbarino, the best-selling author of *Lost Boys*, and Ellen deLara uncover the staggering extent of emotional cruelty and its ramifications and counter the nursery rhyme that words don't hurt.

Reviving Ophelia: *Saving the Selves of Adolescent Girls* by Mary Pipher (**Putnam Publishing Group**, 1994)

Everybody who has survived adolescence knows what a scary, tumultuous, exciting time it is. But if we use memories of our experiences to guide our understanding of what today's girls are living through, we make a serious mistake. Our daughters are living in a new world. The current crises of adolescence — frequent suicide attempts, dropping out of school and running away from home, teenage pregnancies in unprecedented numbers, and an epidemic of eating disorders — are caused not so much by "dysfunctional families" or incorrect messages from parents as by our media-saturated, lookist, girl-destroying culture. The dangers young women face today can jeopardize their futures. It is critical that we understand the circumstances and take measures to correct them.

Your Child: Bully or Victim? *Understanding and Ending School Yard Tyranny* by Peter L. Sheras (**Simon & Schuster**, 2002)

A clinical psychologist and expert in youth violence covers the spectrum of aggressive schoolyard behavior in this eye-opening book, which aims to help readers spot — and stop — a bully, whether it's their own child or someone else's. From the bullies themselves to the bystanders and victims; from how parents can intervene to when they should avail themselves of other resources (teachers, other parents, or professional help) — Sheras has supplied a comprehensive and proactive examination of an increasingly significant topic.

Facing the Schoolyard Bully: *How to Raise an Assertive Child in an Aggressive World* by Kim Zarzour (**Firefly Books**, 2000)

What causes some children to become bullies? Why are certain children targeted for abuse? When and how should parents intervene? What should you do if your child is a bully? What is the school's responsibility? Is there anything you can do to help your child cope? While as many as one-half of children today experience pain at the hands of bullies, parents may still believe that schoolyard bullying is simply a rite of passage, something that must be endured and then becomes a distant memory. But being the victim of a bully can have long-lasting psychological scars.

Playground Politics: *Understanding the Emotional life of the School-Age Child* by Stanley I. Greenspan **(Perseus Publishing, 1994)**

The scary, exciting, dramatic, and often heart-rending experiences of grade school are a critical time in a child's life, with emotional milestones every bit as important as those of the first few years. Yet expert advice to parents usually stops short at the kindergarten door. Now, for the first time, Stanley Greenspan, M.D., one of this country's preeminent child development authorities, offers a "road map" to the stages of normal emotional development during the years from five to twelve. He offers the priceless skills and insight needed not only to keep on course, but to enjoy and marvel at these years of amazing inner growth.

Bullies & Victims: *Helping Your Child Survive the Schoolyard Battlefield* by Paula Fried **(M Evans & Co.,** 1998)

Parents receive an important guide to helping a child survive schoolyard bullying in a title which surveys peer abuse and provides suggestions for parental intervention and reaction. Understand different forms of bullying and different levels of response to its presence through a book written by a professional psychologist and a committee founder.

What to Do ... When Kids Are Mean to Your Child by Elin McCoy **(Reader's Digest Books,** 1997)

One of the more painful parental experiences is watching a child suffer at the hands of other kids and feeling unable to do anything about it. In *What to Do ... When Kids Are Mean to Your Child*, Elin McCoy helps empower parents to help their kids solve the "bully" problem. One of the book's strengths is the way McCoy consistently turns to the children — as well as parents and experts — for advice. McCoy includes six thoughtful and appropriate tactics for kids, as well as additional advice for what parents can effectively do. It's a short book, but it's packed with suggestions, including solutions for sibling problems, what to do when it is *your* child who is mean, how to help your child learn social skills, and where you can go for help.

For more information, visit **www.PublishAmerica.com**...

FOR THE CHILDREN ...
Putting a Stop to Schoolyard Abuse

ADDITIONAL TIPS:

Talk to your kids — Ask your kids what's going on at school. Don't be afraid to talk about bullying if you suspect it. Especially as children get older, they may feel embarrassed or ashamed that it's happening, and you'll need to bring it up. Let them know they have nothing to be ashamed of. It's not their fault.

Take bullying seriously — Often parents think a child may be overreacting, or that what's going on at school is "inconsequential." But it's important to realize that being a target of bullying can affect a child significantly.

Get involved with your PTA or PTO — Find out what's being done at your child's school to stop bullying. Be proactive when it comes to assuring that your child's school has a clear no-bullying policy, and that all staff have been trained in bullying prevention.

Stay with friends — One of the best preventive measures against bullying is developing good friendship skills. Not only does this improve a child's overall self-concept, but when a child is with other kids — especially if there aren't adults around — it's less likely they will be bothered by bullying children.

Act confident — Teach your child to stand tall, holding his head up as he walks, and to look people in the eye when he talks.

Stay safe — Tell your child to try not to be alone in potentially dangerous places such as locker rooms, rest rooms, or empty classrooms.

Ask for help — Teach your child to talk with you or ask a trusted adult at school for help if he or she doesn't know how to handle a situation.

Let your child know that bullying is never okay — Make it clear to your child that under no circumstances is mistreating another person acceptable.

Be a positive role model for your child — You are the most important teacher your child will ever have. Children learn by example — from adults. Be sure to teach your child how to treat others with respect by how you act and speak. Teach your child to be accepting of other people regardless of ethnic background, race, religion, sexual orientation, etc.

Spend more time with your child — Make spending quality time with your child a high priority. Get to know who your child is, what his interests are, and have fun with your child.

Help your child understand how other people feel — Kids who bully have a hard time understanding how others feel. Talk about feelings and ask questions like, "How did you feel when that happened...?" and "How do you think the other person might have felt after that happened...?"

ABOUT THE AUTHORS

Mark and Debra Wein never set out to file suit against the Jefferson County School Board, nor did they ever imagine the matter would eventually go on to become a landmark case in their home state of Rhode Island. All they wanted to do was spare their daughter, Mandi, from the physical and emotional abuse she suffered at the hands of her miniature torturers in the Jefferson County School System.

Simple folks leading a simple life, the Weins never imagined that their daughter was living a hellish nightmare on the pristine grounds of picturesque East Jefferson Elementary School. But soon little Mandi's bruises — not to mention her tears — were just too big to ignore. Seeking refuge from their daughter's teachers, then her counselors, then her principal, then their school board, then their *police*, the Weins were rebuffed at every turn.

From so-called educational professionals who claimed the concerned parents were simply "overreacting" to a callous school board that told them "they would look into it," the Weins found themselves more and more frustrated, even as little Mandi continued to suffer more and more abuse. Eventually, the Weins were forced to pull their daughter from public school altogether and enroll her in a nearby private school — at considerable personal and emotional costs to themselves.

The Weins never set out to be heroes. The Weins never set out to prove right vs. wrong, good vs. bad. The Weins never wanted to be unwitting celebrities. Yet having been through the fire, literally, of a heated court battle that has made them pariahs in their hometown of Jefferson, Rhode Island, the Weins believe that it is finally time to tell their story.

playgroundjustice@yahoo.com

Printed in the United States
1365800001B/295-306

9 781413 700336